7 Principles of Successful and Happy Life

7 Principles of Successful and Happy Life

The Impossible is possible

Alexander
SVIYASH

Leavitt Peak Press

ISBN: 978-1-965679-16-6 (sc)
ISBN: 978-1-965679-17-3 (e)

Rev. date: 10/01/2024

Introduction

WHAT IS THIS BOOK ABOUT? IT TELLS US THAT WE all live in a world of abundance. In our world, there is plenty of food, money, housing, cars, men and women, children, health, love, fame, places for rest and recreation, and more. God created everything in plentitude.

Then why is it that some people have some things in excess, while others in deficiency? Although, if you have a lot of something—for example, money—at the same time, you may not have enough of love or health.

Conversely, if you have lots of love and are healthy, you may be in desperate need of money, etc. Only few people in the world have really everything that they need or want.

We call them lucky, and sometimes we even believe that such people have not fully deserved their success and happiness and that all their success is just a fluke in the eyes of God. These lucky individuals sometimes think so, too, and they do not give much thought that they created their joy and good fortune themselves.

Can any of us become one of the happy people? Yes, if we behave in the same way as successful people.

Everything Depends Only on You!

We will not discover anything new by saying that, in order to achieve success, you should behave as successful people do. This idea is described in detail in numerous books. I will not repeat it again because the authors of those recommendations described *the external behavior of successful people*—the way they work, plan their activities, speak, etc.

To some extent, these recommendations are effective, but *only insofar as the inner world of a reader conforms to the inner world and beliefs in the system of a successful person.* As you understand, there may be a significant discrepancy between these worlds. You may endlessly pursue goals, plan achievements, or work eighteen hours a day. Yet, if deep inside, you consider your boss a fool who takes the wrong place, then you will achieve negative results, i.e., you may be demoted to a lower position or even fired. On the one hand, it seems that you did all a successful person would do; on the other hand, why is there such a failure?

The reason is that, besides the aspects of external behavior, *there exist several other very important rules that we should observe when interacting with people.* These rules are quite simple. If we break them (millions of people do it all the time), life will give us a lesson. Such lessons are not as minor as getting a bad grade for not doing our homework in school. If we do not understand these lessons, Life will block much of our efforts toward achieving our goals. No matter how energetic you are and how hard you try to achieve your goals, you will not accomplish the desired results. You will not become one of Life's favorites, as you will fall far behind, becoming a failure.

On the other hand, if you understand Life's simple lessons and do not violate a few important requirements, you will become a Life's favorite child. As you can imagine, it is very pleasant to be loved by Life. Most of your goals will be achieved without much effort. You will live in inner harmony and joy. You will not be afraid of the future anymore because Life would not harm its favorites.

This might sound like a miracle to you, but it is a reality, and it can always be with you. It only depends on you whether you can easily become one of the most fortunate people.

Someone in the invisible world helps people to observe those easy rules of living in our world. We call this invisible and protecting guardian God, Angels, Heavenly Powers—you name it. Our method is not religious, so we will simply use the notion of "Life," which you can attach to any notion that corresponds to your beliefs.

Some Information about the Author

Readers are usually curious about the author of the book they read, so I will tell you a little about myself. I was born an ordinary family. I graduated from high school, got some work experience, and earned two university degrees.

I did not experience any significant failures or great accomplishments in my life, like the ones you may read about in some books. For example, I did not get my body lethally sick, only to recover later after an immense effort.

I have never been to jail or gone bankrupt, I have never been on the verge of suicide, and the authorities have never been after me. I certainly had problems at work— conflicts with authority figures, which sometimes led to me being fired. I had serious difficulties with my family life that eventually led to divorce. Now I am married again and married happily. So, my life goes on, the way it does for many other people.

The only thing that distinguished me from others was my tremendous curiosity. I always tried to understand why vii everything happens as it does. Why do people face so many problems, why are they always separated by religious, ideological or some other struggle? Finally their lives are often full with suffering and dissatisfaction instead of joy and harmony. Is it actually the right state of things?

Not finding an answer in the books I appealed to the mysticism and ancient esoteric practices. At that time the communism ideology crashed down in our country and we got the opportunity to travel all over the world. I started spending time in India and Nepal, trying to find answers in the old practices. Answers appeared as an insight into the understanding of inner mechanisms which rule human behavior.

After this I transform this knowledge into the books which are comprehensible to most people who want to change their lives.

I spend a lot of time in Nepal, this is my favorite country, where at foothills of Himalayas I get the brightest insights.

Everything I got during such contacts I test on myself and then share with people through my books, lectures and training.

As a result, including the Center of positive Moscow. I am the author of 16 books the printing of which totals in over ten million copies and they are translated into several languages. I have a PhD degree, I'm an active member of the Discovery Academy, and author of several inventions.

I have a wonderful wife and I travel around the world to give lectures and provide training. In short, I created the life that I had wished for myself.

You Can Achieve Everything!

No one but yourself can keep you from achieving the success that you desire. Many people in the world have already used the recommendations offered here, changing their lives miraculously. To illustrate it, let me quote letters that I received from some of my readers.

For several years I have been reading and trying to apply literature on psychology. But your book How to Understand Life's Lessons and Gain Its Favor *has struck me by its grace, accuracy, and scope of information. It replaces dozens of other manuals.* (Leonid Rotstein, Jerusalem, Israel)

I realized with great joy that the book fully reflects my ideas and, even more, my outlook. It is a real pleasure to communicate with people like you. Please accept my deepest gratitude for your books. (Natalia Fligg, North Carolina, USA)

After reading two of your books, I wanted to continue getting to know life and myself. "In the East, simple presentation is considered the best achievement, as simplicity indicates clear understanding." I think that this statement reflects your principles of presentation, and I am very happy about it! I want to thank you and hope you will go on with your work! (Natalia Vasilyeva, Tula, Russia)

Please accept my enormous gratitude for your simple, clear, and understandable books. It is an excellent and clear "Guide to Action" for virtually everybody. (Eugenia V. Romaniuk, Moscow, Russia)

Your book changed my life! Deep from my heart, I would like to thank you, Alexander, and God for sending you to Earth!

Thanks to your wonderful book, I gained a deeper knowledge of Life's laws. You explained why we should act in one way and not in another, and what happens if we act otherwise. (Alexander Barinov, Tver, Russia)

Please accept my sincere words of gratitude for your books! They transformed my life. I feel so peaceful and quiet now! Thanks to you, I realized how strong my Angel is and I want to thank him in writing. Thank you! But it is only the beginning, as I have a strong desire to get to know more about myself and the world, and to correctly achieve my desired goals. (Leonia E. Mellum, Saint-Petersburg, Russia)

With great pleasure, I read your books, which I found unexpectedly, and understood that they are what I need and have been looking for. These books explained in a simple and comprehensible way many of the reasons for my problems that I did not even think of. Several of my friends and acquaintances liked those books, too. They even thought that if they had been published earlier, they could have avoided many mistakes in life.

Thank you for your books! (Pavel Bernatsky, Tambov, Russia)

We could show hundreds more similar quotations from readers' letters, but I think the ones quoted above are self-explanatory.

"Nuts and Bolts" of the Method

In principle, most requirements of human behavior in our world have been well known for a long time. They are the basis of almost all religions. The matter is that in religious texts; the concepts very often are explained in a complicated and not always coherent language, and they never seem to be based on logic that we can easily understand.

Perhaps, it was enough for people living in the past. Yet, today, the principle "trust and do as told" does not work because people want to understand what happens around us and how, finding the reasons why we should observe these exact rules and not some others.

That is why it would be good to translate the requirements of Life into a simple and explainable modern language. I tried to do this in my book.

Our studies show that we have the right and ability to have any of Life's gifts, and we may set any goals and achieve them. Many authors write about it. Unfortunately, these recommendations do not always work, and we found the reason why!

It turns out that, before realizing our desires, we should *start harmoniously interacting with the surrounding world and accept this world as it is*. This means that we should stop condemning what, in our opinions, are the world's certain flaws.

Life starts to bring us joy and anything we want. In this book, we will explain in detail how you can learn to live without grievance and other suffering in our world, which is imperfect in our opinion; you will also learn how to make Life bring you only happiness.

Let's Expand the Borders of Knowledge!

In our view, we cannot exclusively use the notions that we learned at school or in college because the knowledge offered there is always based on science. Science is materialistic— that is, it only considers real things that can be measured, touched, divided into particles, etc. There exist, however, different phenomena in our life that modern science is unable to explain. In the future, science most likely will significantly expand the scope of data about the surrounding world and explain everything it currently denies or considers a miracle. Yet, we are not going to wait for that to happen and will use religious and esoteric (i.e. hidden) knowledge in our reasoning.

Using the information given in this book, any person—even in the most difficult circumstances—can drastically change his or her life to the better (if he or she wants to do so, of course). It is a right. Our book is merely a resource that clarifies why difficult problems arise in our lives and how we create them. We provide you with information, and you arrive at the conclusions on your own. Using this system, many people reconsidered their attitude toward Life.

Consequently, their love life improves, they find money or a job they desire, their business becomes successful, and the illnesses disappear. So we offer you help, and you decide whether you want to use it or not.

If you decide to use my system, you will learn how to fight problems that the ancient people believed were provoked by some "vicious spirits." Yet, we believe that they are provoked by our incorrect attitude to this world.

This Book Is Not Materialistic.

As already mentioned, in our method, we proceed from the fact that besides the visible world—that is, the one that we can touch, measure or, physically see—there also exists an invisible or "unseen" world. The "unseen" world includes everything that we still do not yet know about the environment. In the future, science will probably reveal all the mysteries, but it will not happen soon. We believe that there is another invisible version of our world, and we think we can interact with it to our advantage.

In this book, we will often use the notion of "Life" (i.e., Heavenly Powers, God, the Creator), which merely implies available, invisible powers that influence our reality. There exist many religious, philosophical, and esoteric models of the unseen world. Any of them suits us. Our method does not contain prayers or religious rituals; in this respect, it appears more like a materialistic psychological theory. We also consider, however, practical ways of interacting with the unseen realm, and in this regard, our method is not materialistic at all. That is why both believers and non-believers can use it.

In general, our method is compatible with any religious concept because it stands beyond religion. You can perform the rituals of your faith, using, at the same time, this method because they do not contradict each other.

Field of Use

The information provided in this book explains no more than 80% of the negative events that happen in the world.

The remaining 20% involve people who can be considered "special," and these cases need to be researched and explained.

"Special" people have lives that are different from those of the majority. They are overwhelmingly rich people, famous public figures, show business superstars, serial killers or maniacs, the insane, and those who have been disabled from birth, among others. Their lives and problems are very different from those of most of us. That is why we do not consider these people as much here, and we will be talking more about "us," ordinary people.

We will consider possible reasons behind *typical negative situations* that occur in most people's lives. They include illnesses, failures, family troubles, and other life problems. Our experience indicates that the approach offered in the book can help us to quickly remove these problems forever. This book shows you how to do it without waiting for anybody's help. When all your troubles go away, you will be left with joy only, living your happy and successful life.

No Special Requirements

One of the advantages of the suggested method is that is perfectly tailored to the pace of our modern life. To use it, you do not need to have any special abilities, extra time, or extra space. You can use it at any moment of your free time. You can use our exercises while driving a car, riding a bus, or standing in line. It is very convenient because you do not have to change the usual pace of your life.

"Using the Pronoun Us"

This is a short version of the full Reasonable Path methodology.

This book is he fourth edition of a manuscript written in 1998. It has been a while since then, but people who have not read the book still do not have the lives that they would want. They are not the favorites of Life; they are its stepchildren. They have a real possibility of making their lives more harmonious and successful, and they merely need to reconsider some of their beliefs and rules. That is why many people still need this book.

This book contains the main ideas of what we call the "Reasonable Path" method. Over the past few years, it has gained a lot of support in many countries.

We've shared lots of recommendations and examples of using this approach in different areas, including love and family life, business and work, and solving health problems.

All this information is collected under the general title "Methodology of the Reasonable Path," which consists of more than 10 books.

You can find more information about these books on the Internet at www.sviyash.org. Many people around the world are already using this method, and their lives have changed dramatically for the better. Previously unattainable goals have become realistic for them.

If you like what you read in this book, you can check out the rest of our Reasonable Way method later on and use it to achieve your major goals.

I invite you to make your life more conscious and happy and wish you success along the way!

Alexander Sviyash
www.sviyash.org
2024

1

How to Learn Life's Lessons

IN THE FIRST PART OF THIS BOOK, WE WILL LEARN TO understand what Life wants from us, what lessons it teaches us, and how we can become Life's favorite children. In the chapters to follow, we will tell you what conclusions to draw from these lessons and how to properly use the advantage of being a favorite child of Life.

Different Strategies for Achieving a Goal

How can Life influence our behavior? Very simply—it either helps us or creates obstacles on the way toward our goals.

Everyone has desires and goals in life—to get an education or a gratifying job, earn a lot of money, create a family, raise children, achieve success in a certain matter, etc. We all move toward our goals, and sooner or later, most of us achieve them; however, some people succeed quickly and easily, while for others it takes time and effort.

Let us consider why it happens this way. In theory, two different strategies of achieving any desired goal are possible.

The first strategy is a path of strength, struggle, and overcoming difficulties.

In the animal world, the best analogue is the behavior of a bison or a boar, which are not afraid of anything and tear down all the obstacles on the way toward their goal. Some people act like this in real life, overcoming numerous obstacles with persistence and fervor. It seems that their whole life is devoted to struggle.

They even like obstacles because they allow them to live life to its fullest, as long as these people have good health, of course.

It is clear that, to achieve our goals on this path, we need a great deal of courage, confidence in victory, a lot of energy, and the inborn qualities of a leader. But not very many of us possess these qualities.

The second strategy is a path of calm and confidence in achieving a goal, one that virtually excludes taking part in conflicts, struggle, or overcoming large obstacles. It is a path of a wise man who does not waste his strength struggling against people who do not know what they do.

In the animal world, a wild horse, for example, behaves in this manner. It is strong, but it prefers to listen and look around in case of a threat. This strategy allows the horse to avoid fighting without necessity.

The second path works best for the vast majority of people, who do not possess outstanding inborn leadership qualities. We are going to consider this very path. It means that we will learn to move toward a desired goal, listening to the signals that Life constantly sends us.

Life interacts with us all the time, but we are not accustomed to listening to its hints and giving it the right command. Nobody taught us how to do these things, so we have to make a lot of mistakes, which are the reasons why our desires do not come true.

What Stands in the Way

The main conclusion of our research of the failure when trying to achieve set goals is the following: **The primary reason that we do not fulfill all of our desires is the fact that we are in conflict with the surrounding world or with ourselves.**

But one of the primary conditions for getting practical help from Life **is an ability to accept the surrounding world as it is, despite its obvious, from our point of view, imperfection**.

It is necessary to note that it is very difficult to accept this position in our world, which is constantly being divided into the rich and poor, believers and non-believers, honest and dishonest people, etc. But it is the necessary condition. For you to more easily accept it, let us consider why we come into this world.

1.1   Why Do We Come into This World?

In virtually all religions, we see an indication that a human being should not care about his or her existence and should place this concern with God or other Heavenly Powers. In the Christian New Testament, we find the following precept: "Do not lay up for yourselves treasures on earth, where moth and rust consumes and where thieves break and steal..." Buddhism directly tells us that our world is *maya*, illusion, and there is no necessity to make efforts to achieve success in it; otherwise, we will waste our time and energy chasing a mirage. Similar statements may be found in any other religion.

It is absolutely clear, however, that these statements completely contradict all our convictions and life experiences.

We all know very well that, if we do not do anything at all, one day we will face a serious trouble, e.g., lose our home, job, relatives, or health. Who can be satisfied with this?

Maybe the ancient gave their recommendations concerning some special human beings—for example, monks? It turns out to be untrue. This knowledge relates to everybody. But to realize this, it is necessary to understand why we are born into this world.

To better understand the course of further reasoning, we will accept an assumption that will not influence the following recommendations in any way, but will help better understand their origins.

We will proceed by accepting the existing belief that a human soul can be repeatedly born into different bodies. In oriental religious doctrines, this phenomenon is called *reincarnation*, and it means that some part of us, i.e., our immortal soul, can move into a different body after death.

It happens many times, as many as the soul needs or desires. Let us examine the reasons for this in more detail.

In principle, we imagine that our heavenly substance, the immortal soul, does not need to come to Earth. We could stay for as long as we want in the world that we call "invisible" (in hell or in paradise, according to Christianity). But many of us prefer to travel to Earth and lead an uneasy life.

The Hidden World Has Many Levels.

We know from many sources, including the religious ones, that the hidden world (hereinafter, the "Subtle World") has many levels. It has so many levels because most souls live in very uncomfortable conditions. The lower levels resemble the living places of the poorest people in Africa and Asia. In Christianity, the lowest floors of the Subtle World are called "hell."

At the same time, life on the uppermost floors of the Subtle World is like the life of a very wealthy person living in a private villa on his own island. No doubt, each soul would like to secure a place at a higher level; however, the floor number depends on the amount of "sins" a human soul has committed by the time it leaves the body (i.e., at death). This idea is directly connected to the notion of "karma," which is spread widely throughout the East.

Ancient Eastern Doctrines

The term *karma* is very ancient. In Sanskrit, it means "action." It indicates that, even in the distant past, people understood that their own actions determine their past, present, and future.

Many authors have written about karma, from theosophists and mystics of the past to countless modern writers, and their approach is very different. For the most part, however, they consider karma to be *the burden of problems and illnesses that a human soul inherits in this world.*

In esotericism, they call it "mature" or "family" karma. As a result, readers of those books might feel that their life is predetermined and hopeless. Fortunately, it is not nearly as bad as it seems.

Our experience indicates that most problems in our life result from the mistakes *we make as conscious adults.* We break some of the simple rules that we should observe in this life, and as a result, we face many troubles, illnesses, and even premature death. Not all these difficulties are an outcome of events that happened in our past lives. We ourselves create our problems and illnesses when adopting an incorrect attitude toward our world, and when we pay too much attention to some aspects of our life, completely ignoring the others.

Life is full of diversity, but we rarely accept it. We have ideals, and we are disappointed when our high expectations are not met. In our method, these excessively significant ideas are called "idealizations."

Notion of Idealization

To idealize means to attach excessive significance to an aspect of life that is important to you. This excess manifests itself *in long periods of negative anxiety and stress* that occur when real life does not satisfy your expectations.

For example, you have an idealization when you imagine a certain *behavioral pattern* for your spouse, child, acquaintance, authority figures, or others. You *know* how they should behave, but they act a little (or a lot) differently— that is, *they do not fit the ideals that you imagine,* and their behavior does not match your expectations. As a result, you become aggressive, trying to make them act as you deem appropriate. If they do not behave as you imagine they should, you become depressed or desperate.

In either case, *you do not accept this person* (or the rest of the world), *as he does* not conform to the ideal that exists in your mind.

We also idealize circumstances and events in the world, as well as people. For example, the government acts incorrectly and leads the country into deadlock. Politicians think only about themselves and do not care about others. Religious extremists go crazy and sacrifice human lives fighting for absurd ideas. Life is unfair, and many innocent people suffer in wars and catastrophes, etc.

You yourself can become an object of idealization if for a long time you are unhappy about your appearance, abilities, habits, etc.

There are a lot of these idealizations blemishing our lives.

Open and Latent Idealizations

Before we begin, we suggest that you distinguish between two types of idealizations: open and latent.

We call an *idealization open* when *something in our life annoys us for a long time* (or perhaps provokes some negative feelings). It can be anything: your work, your apartment, a television program, the government, your boss, a co-worker, your mother- in-law, your wife or husband, your child, a significant other, a car, or even yourself. If something annoys you for along time, it means you idealize the object/event and attach excessive importance to it/them because it behaves differently from your point of view, making you unhappy.

It does not matter if you openly show your distress or conceal it charily from other people. It is more important to note that deep inside you have been struggling for a long time, and you feel like you are failing to change the existing order of things.

The second form of *idealization is latent*. It takes place when you are not always aware of being unhappy about something. Sometimes you do not even realize that a certain idea about yourself or other people is very important for you.

If *something extraordinary happens with this idea or person, then deep inside you will be displeased, become aggressive, or feel that your life makes no sense anymore.* For example, you may realize that you cannot live without your great job or family after losing it. Earlier, when you had it all, you did not even think about how important this value was for you, but after losing it, you become conscious of how precious it was. It turns out that deep inside you had idealized that aspect of your life or a person, without noticing it.

To determine your latent idealization, *you might want to try to imagine how you remove different values from your life, one by one.* If the lack of a certain value will not make you suffer emotionally, it means that you do not idealize it and are not obsessed with it; however, if you cannot imagine your life without this value (e.g., job, money, honor, family, children, sex, power, etc.), then you know— you attach an excessive value to it.

You may not even guess that you had a latent idealization until you get in a situation when something unusual happens to whatever it is that is important to you (e.g., you are a very tidy person, and suddenly you find yourself in a dirty and untidy surrounding, which annoys you for a long time).

You Do Not Allow the World to Be Different.

The term excessively means that you value your model of the world too highly, meaning you believe that everyone should (according to your standards) be honest, children should take care of their parents, people should not insult each other, etc., thus not believing that Life can exist in any other variety or form. You think that you know how the world should be arranged, and you are not willing to exercise an idea that it can be different.

Eventually, this value is to be eliminated or taken away from you so that you do not forget that only God can bestow and take away things. He will eventually "confiscate" what you value because you are unhappy about particular order of things in this world, which has been created by God.

Or, on the contrary, you come face to face with a person with values that are alien to you and start a family with him. Or your parents or children have completely different values, and you are constantly experiencing negative feelings, or even trying to forcefully change their attitude towards something that is very important to you.

From a religious point of view, negative emotions are a result of condemning something in the world and can be considered a sin. Consequently, by attaching excessive importance to our expectations and values, we prepare the ground for collecting sins.

So if you are unhappy with the world, i.e., you commit a sin, He shows you your mistake. He does not punish people like slaves, servants, or misbehaving children. Instead, He gives us advice, teaches us, and talks to us as reasonable beings who do not yet understand the obvious truth. As soon as you understand His instructions, He stops defying you.

Life Teaches Us Not to Condemn.

If we idealize something, we will receive a kind of spiritual *"mentoring"*. This mentoring occurs through the *forceful destruction of the value that we idealize*. In this way, Life tells us, "Look, your ideal does not exist anymore, but nothing terrible happened! You are the same and life around you is the same, yet nothing changed! So is it worth it to waste your nerves fighting for your illusions?"

For example, if you are too deeply in love and idealize your partner, then most likely he or she will soon leave you (or fall in love with someone else). Will life end after this happens? Only for you, and only for as long as it takes you to get rid of your suffering. Almost everyone has lived through this experience, and usually more than once.

If you idealize some aspects of family life, it is very likely that your husband, wife, children, or parents will not share precisely the same ideal of it. The same thing will happen in every other matter in life.

To better explain why things happen in this way, we suggest considering the following model.

Stress Accumulator (SA)

Let us imagine *all of the negative emotions* that we feel when life does not satisfy our expectations *as a certain liquid gathering in a container that we will further refer to as Stress Accumulator (SA).*

This liquid flows through an upper pipe into the SA, where it gathers and the level of this liquid shows *the amount of our dissatisfaction with life* in the form of negative emotions. At the same time, the liquid is released through a pipe at the bottom proportional to our good deeds from Life's point of view.

When this reservoir is filled to a particular level (when a certain amount of "sins" has been accumulated), we start to see forced spiritual mentoring—that is, Life proves to us in one way or another that we should not have attached excessive importance to our particular ideals.

There are as many as five ways for Life to show us that our excessive expectations are wrong.

Our World as Purgatory

As we already mentioned, the human soul can just stay in the Subtle World forever and does not need to occupy a human body. Of course, every soul wants to move to a higher level. As we said before, each soul occupies a level according to the amount of liquid in our SA at the moment of the physical death of the body.

It is probably possible for a soul to lower the amount of the liquid in SA while it is in the Subtle World, but doing so would require a lot of time. The probability of the soul doing something good in the Subtle World in order to lower the level of liquid in the collector is very low. It can be accomplished much faster when occupying a human body.

Our planet is a place where we may *lower the level of liquid in our SA over time.* In other words, our planet is a certain purgatory where we can rid ourselves of previous sins. That is why the inhabitants of the Subtle World's *lower levels* very often want to come back to our world to avoid the consequences of their mistakes. Their choices are limited, however, and because of their previous mistakes, they go to countries and families with a lot of poverty, illness, war, violence, and other serious troubles.

This kind of environment makes it terribly difficult to remain serene and forgiving, so it is quite hard for a soul to realize its intention of getting out of the "chronic sinners" circle. If we manage to live under these conditions without bitterness and resentment, however, then the level in our SA will lower radically.

For pure souls inhabiting the *upper levels* of the Subtle World, our planet is a place where they can come to experience real sensations and worldly life, as well as help others to apprehend their mistakes. That is why many peaceful souls return to Earth even when not required.

They choose a body for a new incarnation and come back to Earth with the best intentions. Many of them very likely assume obligations to *bring goodness and serenity, to enlighten and heal people, and to help others achieve the right attitude about life.*

Some inhabitants of the higher levels may ask to come to our world on a tour to feel sensations of the real world and physical body: love, sex, food, interpersonal relations, material wealth, art, and so on. They are most likely born into very rich families, which allows them to enjoy material wealth—that is, of course, if they do not break the required rules, complying with the travelers' code.

Unfortunately, not all of us remember our promises or good intentions when we arrive to our "purgatory." Earthly temptations seize us and we forget *that we had come to this world for a short excursion*—"short" because seventy to ninety years of an average human life is a very brief moment compared to our soul's immortal existence.

Our Life as a Tour

When souls go to Earth for the next incarnation, they are being instructed: "Do not forget that you are going sightseeing, like visiting a museum. Behave appropriately."

That is *why our life is a tour.* It is not a trip to an ordinary history museum where all of the exhibits are put inside glass displays and you can only look at them without touching. Rather, it is a contemporary museum that resembles high-tech museums, where visitors can touch and interact with virtually any exhibit. These exhibits demonstrate different physical effects: echo, interference, diffraction, magnetism, laser radiation, and so on. Visitors can touch the handles and levers, press buttons, and operate any of the exhibits.

By paying the entrance fee to such a museum, we gain the right to employ any of the exhibits within the working hours. We cannot, however, take these exhibits home because they do not belong to us. We come to this museum, play with the gadgets, and leave.

The same thing happens with the human soul. Before it goes to Earth, the soul is told, "We give you a possibility of becoming a human being. Go, look around, and endeavor *everything they have over there.* If possible, get rid of your sins. Please, never forget that you are allowed to stay there for only a limited time. Use everything they have there, but do not break the visitors' regulations and be grateful to the one who let you in."

Those are the rules, and everyone is to observe them.

Unfortunately, our soul usually forgets these instructions. Arriving in the real world, we start considering it *the only one.* Atheism and our education systems teach this idea to us. At the same time, any religion reminds us that this world belongs to God. Only a few of us perceive this important reminder.

For some reason, we do not believe what we are told, and we

become engrossed in this world. We fall passionately in love, thinking that the other person is our property and we cannot live without him or her. Or we become obsessed with money or power. As soon as we become too attached, we forget who created this world and who rules it. We are not even required to love God very much, but rather remember that everything in this world belongs to God and keep this in mind throughout your life.

Take something, experience it, and put it back in its place.

The same principle concerns any excessive attachments, i.e. material goods, spiritual qualities, talents, and creative work. In reality, these rules are sometimes broken. For example, if we have an inborn talent for painting, we may become arrogant and think, "I am outstanding. I am a creator. I am the best!" It is a common and erroneous conviction, and instead of getting rid of old sins, we begin to add new ones. We start attaching excessive importance to our talent and, as a result, experience a lot of distress. An upper valve opens in our SA, and it starts to fill. We come to Earth to lower the level inside the SA, and instead, we increase it.

It is clear that if we gladly use our abilities and do not experience stress, no matter what happens, then we will have no particular problems because we do not need to be "mentored." Sadly enough, this happens very rarely. One way or another, almost all people break the rules of living in our world, and Life has to point them to their errors.

We Are Controlled by a Guardian.

The Creator is most likely too busy and does not have enough time to keep track of all of our thoughts, emotions, and actions. That is why Nature in its wisdom created a certain tool *in our very souls.* This tool *constantly monitors our thoughts and actions* and, on the basis of its observations, regulates the liquid level in our Stress Accumulator.

Later, we will talk about how this tool functions, as well as about the "controller" of our sins. For now, let us call him our Guardian. He monitors our activities, calculates the liquid level in our SA, and decides what to do with each person and how to teach him a particular lesson.

What Happens When SA Gets Filled Up

When our Stress Accumulator *is more than half-empty,* our Guardian does not have any significant complaints about us. We live comfortably, life brings us joy, and our wishes easily come true. It is called a *luck level* and, at this point, Life gladly helps us and makes our wishes come true.

As soon as we start idealizing something and, as a result, feel stressed for a long time, the SA begins to collect the stress liquid. When the accumulator is *two-thirds full,* the Guardian takes measures and teaches us a lesson. He starts sending us reminders, e.g., "You forget that you are just a visitor in this world. Don't think it is all yours, even though you have a ticket. Put things in their places." We begin to receive *strong signals,* and if we do not understand them, the situation becomes much worse.

Actually, subtle didactic signals have been previously sent to us already, but now they are becoming stronger and more consistent. Minor accidents may even happen, depending on the type of idealization—for instance, problems at work, family troubles, financial credit problems, private conflicts, money or property theft, and others.

If we continue to ignore these signals, believing that they are just coincidental, and carry on with our misbehaving, then we will be given a more stringent warning.

Pure accidents do not exist in our world; they are strictly predetermined.

All of the unpleasant things that happen to you are intended by your guardian and are meant to remind you that you have the wrong attitude toward the world around you.

Certainly, you may reject this reasoning and continue thinking that these troubles are mere accidents, yet by doing so, you will be left behind and not experience progress in your life.

If something bad happens—for example, a robbery— you should realize that your Guardian agreed with the thief's Guardian about stealing your money or your car.

This way, *you are reminded of your misconduct and are being penalized for breaking the rules.*

Usually, we do not recognize our Guardian's suggestion and continue our usual way of life. The insurance pays for the stolen car, and you go and buy a new vehicle.

Later, your Guardian pushes you in yet another accident with your new car. It seems like this is the right time to start reconsidering your life, yet it is easier for you to believe that everything was just an accident or the other person's fault; this is because we are stubborn and have only practical reasons for everything. So, Life has to teach us harsher lessons.

When more than 80% of our SA is full, the Guardian starts to send us very strong signals. As we already mentioned, accidents happen, family life is ruined, and serious problems develop at work. First, we lose things *that we are excessively attached to in this world.* A businessman may lose clients, get sued, and go bankrupt, and nothing will seem to work to help improve the situation.

A housewife may face a family crisis, have problems with children or other relatives, and so on.

If we do not understand why these signals are sent, serious illnesses appear. As a result of erroneous ways of thinking, many of us get sick all the time, and it is almost impossible to find absolutely healthy people nowadays.

That is also why illnesses are often accompanied by accidents. In our modern society, medicine rather efficiently fights physical illnesses, and as a result, it is often difficult for the Guardian to make someone sick (especially if you play sports and watch your health). The guardian has, however, plenty of other opportunities to send a warning.

If an illness does not happen, then we face life problems— that is, troubles in many other areas. For example, sometimes very successful athletes attach excessive importance to their fame. They start treating others with arrogance. As you probably guessed, it is an obvious *violation of the rules of tourists' behavior.*

Consequently, an upper valve opens in SA, it begins to fill, and the successful athlete faces troubles in life. He is no longer successful, no one hires him, and people do not talk about him. He thinks his life is over. In reality, he goes through a process when humiliation is cleansing his soul.

Now he is in the same situation as those people whom he recently despised. If he can realize it and asks for forgiveness from Higher Powers, then his situation will soon change to the better.

Usually, we do not fully comprehend the lessons we are taught. We do not understand that it was Life who let us participate in the game and win. It is also Life who changes our lives for the worse to make us understand that we are the same visitors here as the people we despise.

When a soul comes to Earth, *it has permission to play any human games.* It can experience business, love, war, power, politics, spirituality, art, etc. Yet, the soul should not forget that it came to Earth as to a museum or even a *national park.*

Our Life as a Trip to a National Park

We all know that, by paying the ticket, we receive the right to enter a national park, put out a tent there, and if it is permitted, sometimes even hunt. Do not forget, however, that we are under constant supervision. As soon as you break the rules of the national park, a park ranger arrives and makes you pay the fine. If you do something really outrageous, you might be thrown out of the park or even sent to jail.

This example illustrates how we should treat this world. We might dislike something about it, but it should not cause us to become aggressive or get offended. For example, in nature you might dislike that a giraffe's neck is too long or a lion's roar is too loud. You might also detest watching a lion kill an antelope. You might really hate these things, but you understand well enough that nothing can be changed. Even against your will, you must accept this park the way it is.

It is silly to be offended by a giraffe or a lion; however, in reality, we often become annoyed or take offense with politicians, businessmen, relatives, acquaintances, and others. You cannot change the situation; you can only add some sins to your SA by having an incorrect attitude toward things that were not created by you, thus not depending whatsoever on your attitude or your actions.

That is why the best attitude in our life is the attitude of a traveler who came to this world for just some time to enjoy the surrounding, instead of taking critical notes. Again, the world is not created by us, so we have to accept it as is. We are constantly being supervised in case we break the rules determined by this park's owners; however, having come to this life, we do not know, or we forget that there is a guardian who always keeps his eye on us.

This model explains why it helps us to turn to Higher Powers in critical situations. What is a critical situation?

For example, perhaps you were breaking the park's regulations for a long time, so the ranger caught you and wants to send you to jail. Who can save you in this situation? The ranger can hardly help you because he is doing his duty. You can only count on the park's owner, i.e., God. The best way to attract his attention to your misfortune is to tell him about your sincere feelings. God is merciful, so he will probably believe you and forgive you. Of course, he realizes certain insincerity in your Love because you probably rarely thought about God until this critical situation occurred. Just try not to forget the promises you are giving him right now.

God is compassionate, but he does not always have time to forgive your sins.

Your Guardian always supervises you, however. He knows very well how shifty you are, so next time he will put you through such a hardship that you will not even have time to ask for mercy.

That is why re-thinking your values and praying to God is quite efficient in critical situations in general.

What Happens When Your Stress Accumulator Is Full?

Let us continue discussing the Guardian's penalties. When our SA is almost full (90–95%), we face fatal illnesses or major problems (e.g., going to jail). If we still do not understand that we are breaking the rules for visitors and place too much hope in doctors, healers, or judges, then extreme measures will be applied.

At this stage, the SA overflows, and our Guardian loses His patience. If we manage to recognize our mistakes and drastically change our way of thinking and behavior, then the upper valve will close, and the liquid level in the SA will subside. In this case, the illness will go away (we have all heard of cases of inexplicable recovery from AIDS or cancer.) If our views and behavior do not change, our life is taken away from us, resulting in physical death.

When we die, our SA is full, so the soul gets stuck on the lower levels of the Subtle World, almost in hell. No doubt, the soul suffers a lot there. If we idealized something in this life and our life was taken from us as a result, it is at this level that we find themselves among similar souls. If in this life we despised people, then other souls at this level in the Subtle World will despise us as well. Imagine life in the world where everybody despises each other. If we attached excessive importance to sex, then now we share space with sexually addicted people and are being constantly humiliated.

After passing away, we all go to a level of the Subtle World that corresponds to the level of the accumulated liquid in our SA at the moment of death. We create our own hell or paradise by our own decisions. To lower the liquid level in SA, some older people are put in conditions where they lose the ability to have sex, feel the taste of food, and experience other carnal pleasures. This way, by the time we become old, we no longer have so much attachment to the world, and our SA empties a little, even if we do not realize it.

Here we considered a situation of a person who does not realize that he is only a temporary visitor on this planet.

Now let us examine what happens when we do realize that we are only guests on this planet and are allowed here for an excursion.

Conscious Trip to Earth

First, we should buy a ticket. The price is probably a promise to enlighten people and help them. This way, we get an opportunity to empty out our SA if it still contains some stress liquid. Of course, a soul coming from a higher level of the Subtle World has many options concerning the form of its next terrestrial incarnation. To avoid excessive suffering or struggle for survival from an early age, these souls are usually born into prosperous families. You may notice this fact by reading the biographies of many spiritual leaders.

This soul often is given a talent—for example, in sports, arts, science, healing, finance management, trade, etc. These abilities are meant to ease up the existence in this world because, by using them, we become more successful than people without such talents. On the other hand, possessing a talent is also a big test because by being talented, we are more tempted to idealize our abilities, fame, material wealth, etc. If we manage to appreciate our natural abilities, not becoming arrogant and scornful, then we are able to considerably clean out our SA and guarantee ourselves a higher level of placement after our return to the Subtle World.

Unfortunately, the biographies of many renowned painters, poets, writers, scientists, and other famous people show that most of them lead lives full of wrong passions and emotional attachment. As a result, after death, they most likely move two to three levels lower than they were before.

We Have Access to Everything on Earth.

We do not intend any of the above-mentioned discussion to scare you. We can assure you: We come to Earth to use everything offered here. That is why each of us has a chance to try business, politics, love, sex, art, becoming wealthy, etc. We may do any of these things with passion and pleasure.

It is very important, however, to remember that your life is just a game, and you should never despise and hate anyone or take offense. These are mistakes that will lead to the Guardian teaching you a lesson.

How can we determine when we are breaking Life's rules and deserve a reprimand? We believe that everyone should feel it on his own, although we have some recommendations for you. For example, you are fishing and suddenly lose a big fish from the hook. Most likely, you will become very emotional about this failure. Later, you will accept this situation and forgive yourself, the fish, and the rest of the world. You should treat all other failures in the same manner, regardless of whether they concern your family life, work, creative endeavors, etc. It already happened, and we cannot do anything about it. Keep this idea in mind, and you will lead a happy life in which your plans will be worked out quickly and easily.

First Conclusions

Our model of the world and our discussion of the purpose for our coming to Earth explain the reasons for most (not all, of course) illnesses, troubles, and accidents.

Our model supports the idea of other religions that everything in this world belongs to God. That is why we should try not to grieve for a long time if something or someone does not meet our expectations. On the other hand, if we understand how we should behave in this world and accept it as is, we have the right to ask Life to give us everything that we need. We will make our wishes come true because our planet has everything in abundance if we simply allow ourselves these good things to come into our life.

Summary

1. We come to this world and may do whatever we want here (of course, without causing harm to others). At the same time, we should not consider anything our own and idealize any terrestrial values. We are just visiting this world briefly and should consider our successes and failures as a part of the game.

2. If we start attaching excessive importance to some material or spiritual values, i.e., idealizing them, our Stress Accumulator (SA) will overflow, and Life will give us spiritual lessons, which will destroy the values that we are excessively attached to and prove that our convictions are illusory.

3. If we do not understand these signals and continue breaking the rules of this world, we face an early death.

4. If we reconsider our attitude toward life and people and stop attaching excessive importance to our expectations and ideas, then Life does not need to give us its lessons anymore because we have already learned them. As a result, we may get rid of serious illnesses, troubles, accidents, and other things that hinder our life.

1.2 Stress Accumulator

Let us remind you that we consider the SA a *reservoir that collects human stress—"sins."* We can imagine that our SA collects them in the form of a stress liquid. A model of SA is shown in Figure 1.

As you see, each valve corresponds to a different idealization. If we possess an idealization, a corresponding valve opens in the upper pipe, allowing the stress liquid to flow into the SA.

It is important to say that by "sins," we do not mean thoughts and actions that are considered sinful by usual moral and religious norms. The cause of various problems in our lives, which is primarily responsible for causing different problems in our lives. This discontent with life causes the stress liquid to enter our SA.

Remember that *an idealization* of some material or spiritual aspect begins when we *attach excessive importance to it,* regardless of whether we actually own something already or only dream about having it. When something in the world does not meet our expectations, *we experience prolonged stress.*

Idealizing Earthly and Spiritual Values

The SA pipe collects our sins *(i.e., earthly and spiritual idealizations).*

These sins often take the form of excessive attachments to the following aspects of our life.

1. **Money and material values.** Most of us do not have enough money or material goods, and this situation is normal because our desire to have money motivates us to strive toward our various goals. The idealization takes place only when your income causes you to continually experience stress and you believe that it is not enough for a decent existence.

2. **Beauty and attractiveness.** This idealization exists if you constantly worry about your appearance, whether you

are beautiful enough, you have a nice figure, you are well dressed, your hair is well done, etc.

3. **Work.** Many people are "workaholics" and cannot imagine life without their beloved profession. As a result, Life periodically teaches such people lessons in the form of workplace troubles or even job loss.

Stress Accumulator

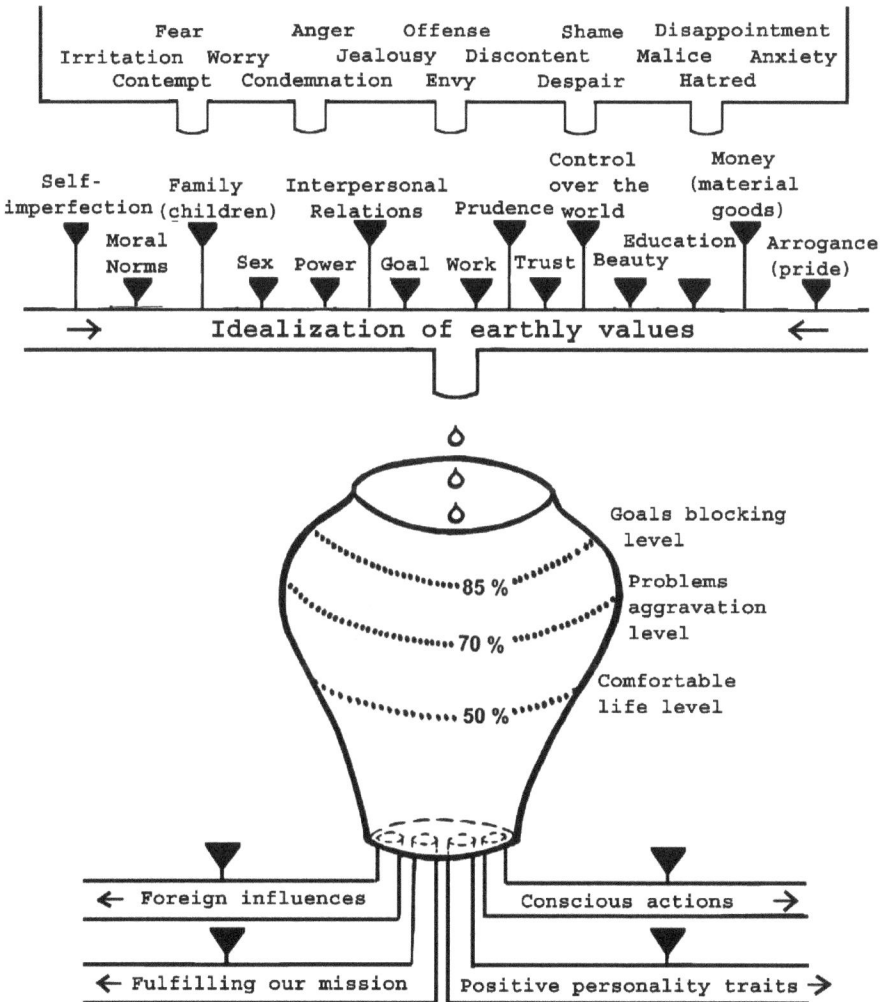

Fear	Anger	Offense		Shame	Disappointment
Irritation	Worry	Jealousy	Discontent	Malice	Anxiety
Contempt	Condemnation	Envy		Despair	Hatred

Self-imperfection	Family (children)	Interpersonal Relations	Prudence	Control over the world	Money (material goods)

Moral Norms		Sex	Power	Goal	Work	Trust	Education Beauty		Arrogance (pride)

→ **Idealization of earthly values** ←

Goals blocking level

85 % Problems aggravation level

70 %

50 % Comfortable life level

← Foreign influences   Conscious actions →

← Fulfilling our mission   Positive personality traits →

4. **Family and children**. This idealization occurs when you are convinced that you are supposed to have a family and children but have no idea about how your spouse should behave behave or about family relations and duties, your children's education, and so on. When someone close to us has a different opinion on those issues and does not want to meet our expectations, we become depressed for a long time.

5. **Sex**. In your dreams, you can have sex with many women (or men), but in reality, you do not experience intimacy because of shyness, distrust, etc. You constantly wonder if you are a good lover, and you attach excessive importance to sex. Or on the other hand, you consider sex a big sacrifice or even a humiliation.

6. **Power.** Many of us love power, but not all of us have an opportunity to exercise it. Men mostly try to become powerful in their home environment or at work, while women pursue power mostly in family life. Power is a good thing; it helps to rule people. Idealizing power takes place when we crave it and enjoy using it to humiliate.

7. **Faith and trust.** Many people have sacrificed their lives trying to build upon the ideas of others (democracy, monarchy, communism, etc.). At present, many people believe in these ideas and become annoyed when reality turns out to be different. *Excessive trust in others* also falls into this category. People will try to destroy your ideal and will not justify your excessive trust in them.

8. **Moral norms.** This kind of idealization is most common among older people who were raised according to the older times standards. As a result, they become annoyed with what seems, from their point of view, the immoral behavior of young people—the weakening of moral values and many other changes in life.

9. **Relations.** This idealization takes place when we have a distinct idea about the way people should behave in general.

It means they should be honest, fulfill their obligations, be kind to other people, never lose temper, etc. When we find ourselves in an environment where people do not behave according to our ideal, we get angry.

10. **Development, education, and intellect**. The idealization of these qualities is typical of scientists, artists, and academic people. It makes them despise uneducated people or those who can be perceived as "underdeveloped." This idealization can manifest in a person who condemns himself or herself for a poor education.

11. Behavior of others. We think that all people are sensible and that it is always possible to come to an agreement and explain everything to them. The more stubborn they seem about their delusions, the more we suffer from their behavior.

12. **Self-imperfection**. This idealization occurs when we constantly judge ourselves for lacking important qualities (determination, purposefulness, good ancestry, connections, education, etc.). The other symptom of this idealization is having a phobia of making a wrong decision. As a result, it takes ages for us to decide anything.

13. **Our success**. This idealization makes us exaggerate our achievements, overly praise our success or professionalism, and be reluctant to listen to anyone's advice. When people with such idealization are not successful, they blame their problems on other people and circumstances. They take offense easily and react aggressively to any critical remark when other people doubt the correctness of their actions.

14. **Goal.** This idealization exists when we are determined to achieve something, we get annoyed by any obstacles or delays. It really does not even matter whether we may become nervous or blame ourselves or other people—we just cannot tolerate that our goal has not been achieved.

15. Some of us believe that we are the center of the universe. Whatever happens in the world, it works either against us or for us. As a result, we only value our own opinions, needs, and interests, and we despise other people.

16. This attitude toward the world is typical. As part of their job, they develop major planning, and they become annoyed when their business strategies do not work out. Therefore, they do not trust anyone and try to do everything themselves. In family life, this idealization takes place in the form of one spouse's authoritarian behavior (trying to impose his or her will on others). People sometimes referred to as "control freaks" may constantly worry about their family members or be afraid of the future.

Other idealizations exist in addition to those previously mentioned, and even include being excessively religious. Of course, there is nothing wrong with having an excessive faith in God, except some believers judge and despise non-believers or people belonging to other religions.

Some of them even take offense with God for not paying enough attention to them.

Let us return to our SA model. Each of the previously considered idealizations has its own valve connecting to the pipe, and as soon as we experience long-term suffering as a result of our failed ideas, the valve opens and the stress liquid starts to flow through the pipe into the SA.

As long as we idealize even one earthly value, the appropriate valve stays open and allows liquid to pour through the pipe further into the SA. As soon as we realize that we have the wrong attitude toward this value, the valve closes and the stress liquid stops entering the SA. If all of the other valves are also closed (i.e., if the person does not have any other idealizations), the liquid level starts leaving through the lower pipe, Life stops giving this person spiritual "penalties", and his situation starts improving quickly.

Cleaning the SA

There are several pipes at the bottom of the SA. These pipes remove the liquid from the SA, thus cleaning it. The SA is cleaned when we repent our sins through our thoughts and actions.

The pipes at the bottom are always half open allowing the stress liquid to drip slowly out. This conclusion is drawn from the following observation: As soon as the liquid stops coming in, the SA starts to gradually empty because the number of accumulated "sins" goes down.

The SA empties through the following four pipes:

Deliberate Good Actions

One of the lower pipes deals with deliberate good actions. We may idealize some earthly values, but by performing good actions and by having a good attitude toward other people, we can open a valve on that pipe and let the fluid escape. Or prevent it from reaching the critical level in SA.

Deliberate good actions include compassion, mercy, unselfish work toward noble goals, charity, self-sacrifice, and similar examples meant for the good of other people.

For example, if you give this book to a friend who is experiencing difficulties, it will count as a deliberate good action.

Personal Positive Traits

The second lower pipe deals with positive personal traits of character, such as kindness, good nature, cheerfulness, optimism, etc. We can be very attached to something, i.e., have many idealizations, but thanks to having a good character and optimistic attitude, our SA never becomes full. Many good-natured people fall into this category.

The Influence of Others

The third pipe at the bottom of the SA concerns the *influence of other people.* For example, anyone they can remove some liquid from the SA. *The results most likely will be short term* because without closing the pipes at the top, the SA will become full again quite soon (in a week, a month, or a year). That is why some healers use their influence to remind patients to take their medications for their existing illnesses. Medicines only help while we take them, but as soon as we stop, our problems return.

The same principle applies to religious purification rituals. For example, Christians use fasting and confession. The priests understand this principle very well and ask people to confess every week. These methods are effective for believers, and they should be preformed consistently.

Fulfilling Our Mission

Another pipe at the bottom of the SA concerns *recognizing and fulfilling the mission that brought us to this world.*

We all have several tasks to perform in each of our incarnations (e.g., to create a family, give birth to a child, become a warrior or scientist, invent something new, or gain new knowledge). It seems that we *have to try everything in this life*—love, family, power, politics, teaching, sports, war, intellectual pursuits, and so on. *Some people fulfill several missions in the course of one life.* A clear indication of this fact is a *sudden change in our field of activity.*

For example, we work as a cook or teacher, and we are good at it and achieve great success. Suddenly, without any obvious reason, we quit and begin pursuing something absolutely different—for instance, we become a farmer or an artist. Having reached success and satisfaction in one field, we want to succeed in something new. Today, there are many people like this.

For its next incarnation, our soul can choose any task that it was unable to fulfill in this life. For example, its mission may be to create a new work of art or increase scientific knowledge, to create a perfect family, or to organize people's work into a new enterprise. As a result, the soul gains new experience and takes another step toward its spiritual growth.

Unfortunately, we do not usually remember what kind of task it is that our soul had wanted to pursue; however, the situation is not so bad. We are often attracted by *a certain type of activity* (e.g., social or political affairs, business, teaching, medicine, technology, or the arts). If we are satisfied with our work, we *succeed and are happy with our destiny*, deriving pleasures from our life. This happy feeling indicates that we are on the correct path toward fulfilling our soul's mission.

If we fulfill our mission in life and enjoy what we do, the valve on the lower pipe opens, and the liquid slowly seeps out from the SA.

Empty SA

At some point, the SA of a certain person may become *empty*. An empty SA indicates that this person has no stress liquid or "sins." He is not attached to anything on Earth (in the wrong way) because no event or circumstances can cause him stress or provoke his negative emotions. He accepts this world as is. He usually has correct convictions and helps people by healing, giving sermons, and living his life. No one sends him negative energy, and even if someone does, it has no power or influence over him.

Nothing holds this person on our planet; *he stays only for as long as he wishes and can leave at any moment.* Whenever they wish, these individuals can travel to the Subtle World and return to the human body. There are not many humans of this kind in our world, e.g., yoga adepts of high initiation or highly spiritual people. When they conscientiously realize that they have fulfilled their mission, they leave our world, regardless of their age.

One way to achieve this state is through a conscious renunciation of earthly values, called asceticism; however, this way is hardly acceptable for people living an ordinary life because the reality provokes us to care about our relatives, to earn money for paying our bills, and so on. It is extremely difficult to abstain from negative stress when we do our usual business, which is why most of our SA never empties out fully.

Here is the way most of us can clean our SA: Each of us *should figure out which of the valves is open* and if we had any events in our life that could be considered lessons that we were taught as a result of having an incorrect conviction or idealization. Most likely, each of us can find more than one event of this kind in our life.

We suggest [that you] analyze willfully your life, determine what ideals you have concerning this world, and calculate the stress liquid level in your SA. We will help you to do this kind of evaluation in the next paragraph.

Summary

1. The SA is filled with your idealization of earthly and spiritual values. The pipes at the top of your SA give the liquid that characterizes your incorrect attitudes toward this world.
2. By knowing the principles of filling and emptying our SA, we can consciously regulate the level of the stress liquid, thus controlling our destiny and health.

1.3   Self-Diagnosing the Negative Liquid Level in Your SA

In this section, we will explain how you can determine the level to which your SA is filled and how you should behave and deal with your life in the future.

The First Stage of Self-Diagnosis

The first step of self-diagnosis is to evaluate the load of sins you had before coming to this world. In other words, you need to determine which level of the Subtle World your soul occupied (how full your SA was at the moment of your birth). Most people come to Earth with at least some liquid inside their SA.

Mature karma determines our future birth conditions, character traits, habits, etc. The more positive we were in our past life, the less liquid we had in our SA at the moment of death and the more opportunities we will have when we return to Earth.

To make it easier, let us *divide the Subtle World into ten levels.* At each level, souls live in different conditions. Let us call the first floor Hell and the tenth floor Paradise, even if this model sounds too simplified.

At the first stage of your self-diagnosis, you need to determine approximately *how full your SA was at the moment of birth.*

It is convenient to measure the liquid level in some *quantitative index*—for example, by the percent to which the SA is full. Let us assume that a full SA equals 100% (the SA of a sinner who seriously violated the rules of living in this world for a long time.) On the other hand, an empty SA is 0% full, and it is an SA of a saint who came to this world with his own mission and did not judge the world where he lived. We call such a person blessed.

At the moment of birth, our SA is about 15–25% full. You can approximate the level according to the following indications:

1. **Country of birth**. If you were born in a country with a stable economy and political system (e.g., Western Europe or the United States), it means that your soul had a wide choice that only souls living at the higher levels of the Subtle World have.

2. **Family**. Some of us are born into extremely rich families, while others have illiterate, poor, alcoholic, or drug-addicted parents. So, some people live a happy life, while others suffer. The better your soul behaved in the past, the more opportunities exist for your soul to choose a good family in this life.

3. Cultural and educational level of your parents. The souls living on the higher levels of the Subtle World are most likely to choose parents with the highest level of education and who work in the fields of administration, science, or art.

4. **Your health after birth**. If you were born healthy, it means that your SA was not full when you died in your past life. If you suffer from some inborn illnesses, however, your soul came from the lower levels of the Subtle World.

5. **Destructive personality traits**. No doubt, we all possess a wide variety of character traits. Some people are quiet and balanced, while others are highly emotional, touchy, cruel, soft, or depressed. We brought all these personal traits with us from our previous lives, and they show that in the past we were seized by many passions, especially if these traits correspond correctly to our signs of Zodiac and astrological forecasts. The presence of these traits is directly connected to the level of the stress liquid in our SA.

All of this shows us something about our past lives. By using these indicators, you can approximate how full your SA was at the moment of your birth.

Approximating the Liquid Level in Your SA at Birth.

A healthy and talented child born in a rich and happy family has a low starting liquid level in his SA (approximately 5–6%).

A healthy baby who is born in a country with a strong economy, and who has educated parents and good living accommodations and an average family income, has a higher liquid level (10–12%).

A child born into a poor family with uneducated parents with no stable job has an estimated liquid level of 15–18%.

If a baby has a serious inborn disease, his SA is 20–25% full at the moment of birth.

Based on these figures, you can approximate the level of liquid in your SA for yourself.

While evaluating the liquid level in your SA at the moment of birth, do not exaggerate its importance at older age. As you grow older, the situation changes according to your thinking and way of life.

Higher standards for "saints"

The conditions we have considered so far refer only to the "starting conditions" of your existence in this world. The greater the load you have brought with you from past lives, the more difficult your life will be.

It seems that a person who comes to Earth with almost full SA is already in the worst possible situation and can't do anything about it.

If we come to Earth from higher levels of the Subtle World, we should be careful because it is much easier to fall down than to rise up. People who come from higher levels have better starting conditions in life, and it is easier for them to achieve prosperity and success on Earth if they do not violate the "visitor's code".

However, they are held to much higher standards, and if they start idealizing something, their SA fills up much faster than other people. This goes some way to explaining why talented people who lead colorful and emotional lives (musicians, actors, poets) very often die young.

On the other hand, people who live monotonous unemotional lives can physically live much longer in our world.

So, we have assessed our starting conditions in life. Now we need to determine what our SA looks like now. We can do this on our own, without resorting to the help of fortune-tellers and clairvoyants.

The second stage of self-diagnosis

We have come to the second stage of our reasoning, and it is time to determine how full our SA is at present. One way of accomplishing this task has already been given by us earlier in our consideration of the structure of the SA. As the stress fluid (your "sins") collects through the valves (i.e., idealizations) into your SA, you should think about each of them separately. In this way, you can determine which idealizations you currently have. Using this method is quite simple.

How to determine if you have idealizations

If you remember, having an idealization means that you have been stressed about something for a long time (for example, a husband who is not successful enough, a wife who is not very sexy, a child who misbehaves, or the illness or death of a loved one).

Try to remember what problems and situations make you suffer the most and determine if your stress is caused by idealizing some earthly value.

If you haven't been sad about anything in a long time, consider whether you have any hidden idealizations. You need to visualize your life without certain components: love, family, money, health, work, understanding, fame, etc. These are the things we may place undue importance on. If you can imagine life without each of these, or a few of them, and if their absence does not make your life empty or aimless, then you have no idealizations. You are a saint, and you have no business being in this world.

Life is a game.

Most people discover one or more values that they cannot live without (e.g. family, children, love, work, money, etc.). If you are one of these people, the valves corresponding to these values are open and negative stress enters your SA. These idealizations bring you illness, trouble and conflict.

We are not asking you to completely renounce these values, because life without them may become meaningless to you. We are simply suggesting that you reconsider these values.

Try to consider them in the context of achieving victory.

If something doesn't work out the way you hoped or a problem arises, consider it a temporary loss, not the end of life. Keep playing the game and try to win.

We will talk more about this attitude in chapter three of this book.

Indirect "Lessons"

We cannot literally look into our SA and see how full it is.

We can, however, make this determination by paying attention to some *indirect signs*. Remember that our Guardian *takes measures according to the level of our discontent with Life*. Unlike doctors and clairvoyants, our Guardian never makes mistakes. We know from our life what lessons our Guardian is giving us, so by considering them, we can evaluate how discontented we are with our life and even understand which valves in our SA are open.

Our Guardian can educate us by sending troubles our way, destroying our plans, giving us professional or family problems, keeping us from enjoying a love life, or making us ill.

There is no particular order for these measures. They are chosen individually according to our idealizations or misconceptions. (Small problems and illnesses happen to all of us, however.)

Approximating the Current Liquid Level in Your Stress Accumulator

We suggest that you take a look at the recent negative events of your life, and based on their significance, evaluate the liquid level in your SA. Let us consider several possibilities, beginning with the most serious:

1. If you are suffering from a fatal disease (e.g., cancer or AIDS) or if you are in jail for a serious crime, your SA is 92–96% full.
2. If you have an illness that is serious but not lethal, the level of stress liquid in your SA is a little lower (up to 90%).
3. If you are involved in a serious car accident, fire, robbery, or a lengthy trial, or if all of your plans fail and you continually face problems, your SA is 80–90% full.
4. If you face financial problems, you have bitter family relations or sexual troubles, or important business is moving forward too slowly and it takes all your time and energy (in a negative way), your SA is 70–80% full. These difficulties do not lead to death, but they keep spoiling your life.
5. If everything works out just fine for you, but could be even better, then your SA. This result is positive, but try not to make it worse.
6. If your life brings you joy and all your dreams come true the way you want, the liquid level in your SA does not exceed 50%.

7. People in their SA are the ones involved in spiritual, educational, or charitable activities.

Ask your subconscious mind

We have looked at a way to logically assess the level of stress fluid in our SA. This is a comprehensive method that works well.

Summary

1. Each of us is able to determine how many "sins" we brought with us from past lives to calculate the current level of stress fluid in our SA.
2. The following indicators help to determine the level of stress fluid in our SA: country and place of birth, family, health status at the time of birth, and innate character traits.

1.4   Typical "Educational" Measures

This task is difficult because it is hard for us to evaluate ourselves and accept that some of our views are wrong, especially if we have held these beliefs for many years.

Without accepting our errors, we will be unable to calculate correctly the level of the stress liquid in our SA, and we will not be ready to learn the lessons that our Guardian prepared for us to correct our mistaken views.

As you understand this already, these measures can be quite painful.

Keep it in mind that the idealization of earthly and spiritual values can be corrected by situations that destroy these values. We can be certain that our Guardian *correctly "diagnoses" our mistakes and provides us with the correct "medication."* Consequently, if we analyze the educational measures that we face in our life, we can determine their reasons.

There is only a certain number of educational measures, so we can define the most common ones and classify them according to the different aspects of our lives.

The *primary "educational" categories* are family, children, and work. Let us examine each of these categories.

1.5 Typical Lessons for the Family

Remember that our SA is not empty when we come to this world. Instead, it is filled with erroneous views that we bring with us from our previous life. Normally, we do not change our views while we are in the Subtle World because it provides us with only limited opportunities for purifying our soul. For this purpose, we come to this world; however, we bring our wrong viewpoints with us to this world, and Life is aware of it.

To improve the growth of our soul, Life in advance plans particular situations of our arrival to this world—the situations that will help us to destroy our erroneous notions. One of the common situations when this occurs is our family life. Let us take a look at the *family relations* between a husband and wife. As you observe it yourself, many families lack mutual understanding to some extent or another, which often results in offense, arguments, scandals, and finally divorce. Why does it happen?

It means that the excessively important values of one spouse are destroyed because the other one denies them. This explains most of the conflicts between spouses and the lack of understanding in many people's family life.

Of course, not all of us have idealizations that can be destroyed in the context of family life. As a result, some families have happy lives without many arguments or much mutual discontent. Yet, these families represent the minority.

Most people idealize such *family values* as fidelity, without stress, and so on. As you might guess, these qualities are most common in women because they are more apt to pay excessive attention to these values.

When women idealize these values, men have nothing else to do except to destroy them. Men are forced to drink, go fishing, have affairs spending a great deal of money on mistresses, spend excessive time at work or with friends, and so on. To fulfill their educational family mission, men have to do things that public opinion deems immoral. As we already noted, however, there are sometimes discrepancies between moral norms and the necessities of spiritual learning.

Women are not the only ones who idealize family values. Most men idealize these values, too. A man's *family idealizations* are often manifested in jealousy, in trying to control the behavior of the wife and children, and in attempts to plan the family budget on his own. These values must be destroyed, and women are the instruments to fulfill this task. As a result, women look for love affairs, spend too much money on shopping, neglect their household chores, etc. This way the *spouses give each other all kinds of spiritual lessons.* When one side does not understand these lessons, the other side takes offense, and they may get divorced.

Let us see how Life is able to pair people who will destroy each other's values.

Therefore, before getting married, we can see that our future partner has different views on life, and we have a choice not to marry him/her. Yet, in reality, things rarely turn out this way.

Love

To pair people with opposing values, Life invents a method for depriving us of what seems to make sense to us. It is called love. *Love may be considered a way of diminishing our intelligence for enough time for us to marry our spiritual "teacher."*

To make us feel better, love is supposed to be very pleasant, and we can fall in love more than once in our lifetime. That is *why marriages based on passion are usually marriages between people who need to destroy each other's excessive values,* i.e., between people who idealize different values in life (e.g., a wife who adores tidiness and material wealth, and a husband who loves soccer and his own independence).

Life is very good at coupling people, so by knowing one of the spouses, it is easy to predict the character traits of his partner.

If a husband is very prudent and logical, he is most likely going to choose an emotional and hot-tempered wife.

If a wife loves money and believes that her husband should have a high salary, her husband will most likely be broke or pay no attention to money at all.

If a husband values sex very much, his wife will not be particularly interested in it.

If a wife is very well mannered and is critical of rude people, she is very likely to fall in love with one.

If a husband has strict ideas about raising a child, his wife will have the opposite ideas. If a wife likes one type of food, her husband will prefer a different

If one partner really loves his/her relatives, the other one will not care much about keeping good relationship with them.

Yet, in this process, we destroy each other's idealizations and, in a way, help develop each other.

A wife does not realize that her husband is her "spiritual educator" who stops her from idealizing earthly values, and vice versa. To make this "treatment" last longer, a child is born into this family. Children usually connect people and do not allow them to divorce too early. They also participate in "spiritual education" and often destroy the values of one or both of their parents.

Marriage Problems

Now let us talk more about love, particularly about the cases when people fall in love but do not get married. This situation arises *when a woman or a man is not able to find his or her "better half" to create a family.* Women in this situation are believed to suffer from what is called a "celibacy crown," and some healers try to help them to get rid of this "infirmity." What does this "crown" mean from the point of view.

It is easy to understand that this problem is caused by *excessively idealizing family life.* A woman can idealize family life so much that

Life cannot find for her a husband who would match her ideal, but on the other hand, could teach her the proper "lessons." Actually, it is not so difficult to find a proper man who could become an "instrument of her torture;" there are plenty of them around.

The reason is that it is difficult for Life to make the girl so foolish that she could fall in love with such a guy and marry him. The prospective partner is so different from her ideal of a husband that her emotions cannot win over her common sense and make her do such a "crazy" thing.

Some women have too much common sense and do not listen to their emotions. In these situations, Life is unable to deliver her the right partner; however, she does not deserve a better one because he would be unable to give her the proper lessons. That is why she has to wait till the next incarnation to fall in love and have a family.

As you can see, Life cannot always use love as a "treatment." If we excel at logical thinking, imagining exactly what we want from life and from our partner, then it is difficult for our Guardian to make us unreasonable enough to fall in love with the wrong person. Usually it happens with *more mature people.*

People normally get married at a young age, when they are not wise enough and are mostly driven by their emotions.

If Life wanted, it could make us fall in love with a person who will cause the most destruction to our life.

The more idealizations that we have about love, the worse the person we will marry. Life is life. Many books tell us stories about these kinds of marriages.

Reasonable Choice of a Spouse

Now let us consider cases when *we do not marry a person who we love* or we divorce our "spiritual teacher" after the spell of love disappears, and as a result, we do not learn the lessons that Life intended to give us through that person.

These events indicate that our idealizations have not been destroyed and our SA still remains full.

In these cases, we usually look for a new partner using our common sense. As a result, it is difficult for our Guardian to find us a partner with a value system opposite to our own (what we spiritually need), and we choose a person with interests common to ours and whose character traits are compatible with ours. Does this mean that we will not receive more lessons from life?

If we bring our erroneous beliefs into our adult life and find a partner who idealizes the same values, then Life will teach both of us. In this case, however, Life has fewer choices of educational measures. Here are the possible ways to destroy the idealizations of both spouses:

1. A child who ignores the values cherished by both parents
2. Loss of property (e.g., family bankruptcy)
3. Illnesses that require great effort from both spouses.

For example, the common idealization of material well-being may be destroyed by removing money and other material values from your life in the form of money loss, minor car accidents, property theft, etc. If these lessons do not teach you anything, the situation will become more serious. Your house may get robbed, the car may be seriously damaged, the house may be ruined by fire and insurance companies may be indisposed to compensate the loss, etc. These events exemplify the most simple and common lessons. Actually, the Guardians of the couple might work together and do something much worse to the spouses to destroy their idealizations.

Life is life—let us repeat it once again. We have to observe its rules.

Scandals Are Good for You.

Let us talk about scandals that often accompany some people's family life. What are the reasons for conflicts and how should we behave when someone makes us angry?

Scandal Is a Way of Exchanging Energy.

There are several aspects to this issue. From a spiritual point of view, each scandal helps *transfer energy from one person* (the energy donor) *to another* (the energy vampire).

In most cases, scandals take place when one person lacks the energy usually received from food, air, and the environment. As a result of some inner disorder or ailment, this person's body lacks energy, but he or she does not want to be sick or die.

Therefore, this person's body starts looking for another way of gaining energy. It is possible to acquire it *from other human beings*, especially from very emotional ones. It does not matter if this energy is negative or positive. That is why some people (mostly the elderly) provoke others to anger. They use any means necessary (admonition, insults, criticism, tactless statements, etc.). Everything works to make you angry, thus making you lose you energy to feed the "vampire."

After screaming and exchanging insults, both parties would have to come down to a quiet state. The "donor" feels as if he has no more energy to continue with the argument. The "vampire" is content because he collected some energy that he can run on for a certain period of time. Try to remember some scandals in your family, and ask yourself if this scenario sounds familiar to you.

This notion explains how a scandal manifests itself *at the energy level* and also how it is explained by clairvoyants and healers who use energy for their work.

We need to realize *the reason why the "vampires" lack long-standing energy.* For now, we will try to set aside such reasons as illnesses, lack of sleep, or fatigue, which are only an outcome of those reasons. Most likely, the real reason is the effect of the *"lessons" taught to us for having the wrong attitude toward life.*

Older people, especially the ones who did not achieve much in life, often criticize others (the young, the wealthy, or the healthy); they get upset with life and impose their ethics and standards on others. Their Guardians have to teach them "lessons." As a result, those people do not receive sufficient energy, and they look for an alternative energy source, such as pulling it from other people.

Scandals Help Us Stand for Our Principles.

If you do not have any idealizations, it is virtually impossible to engage you in a scandal.

Nothing will bother you because you are emotionally well balanced.

If your opponent finds a way to make you lose your temper, you should be grateful to him. He helps you *find a value to which you attached excessive importance.* He helps you to reveal your erroneous beliefs so that you can get rid of them.

These beliefs can include your point of view about your children's education, politics, your appearance or intellect, or any other value. Each of us has our own set of principles that a "vampire" will use trying to push all available buttons to make us angry.

On this account, scandals are useful for our own good because they become an excellent diagnostic tool to see all our idealizations and to offer us the right treatment. The "vampire" destroys our idealizations by his behavior, convictions, or actions against us, so let us be grateful to the person who drags us into a scandal.

Keeping this in mind, we can decide *our own role in the approaching conflict.* There are several options.

We may *try to avoid the conflict,* i.e., remain silent, leave, or try to bring some levity by a joke. In this case, the "vampire" will not receive the necessary vital energy and will continue grating on our nerves, or if it fails, he will switch to a different person (a sensitive child, a nervous neighbor, an irritated housewife, etc.).

We can yield to *the "vampire"* and allow him to pull us into a conflict. If we are able to control our anger, it will not hurt us much, and it will totally satisfy him. A couple of days later, however, we will find ourselves in the same or similar situation again.

Besides actively participating in the conflict, we can use other tactics. For example, we *may show compassion to the person who provokes us*: mentally wishing him respect, appreciation, higher self-esteem, etc. By doing so, we will still feed him part of our energy, a different kind though—instead of the anger energy he expects, we will give him the energy of love and forgiveness.

Hopefully, the "vampire" will be able to absorb it—in which case, his reaction might be quite surprising to us.

He may apologize or even cry from remorse. If this energy is still not enough for him, he will attempt to further provoke our anger.

Actually, some "vampires" prefer this *energy of compassion and mercy*. To receive it, they often provoke you for a pep talk.

There are other solutions to the problem. If we want to *really stop conflicts*, it is necessary to restore the energy of the sick person (the "vampire"). It is only possible if he will change his attitude toward the world and will be able to comply with Life's important requirements in order to stop judging the world and start accepting it as is.

Family Idealization

Now let us study *our family life* in light of the aforementioned explanations. Try to evoke what particularly *annoys you about your spouse*, what he or she does wrong according to you. It may concern the aspects of housekeeping, sex, money spending, specific character traits, or the like. You have to realize that *you idealize those exact qualities*, i.e., you attach excessive importance to them.

You are taught lessons for these idealizations because they cause your Stress Accumulator to fill up. The more you are discontent with some qualities of your partner, the faster your SA becomes full.

Now try to remember *which of your own traits or habits annoy your spouse the most.* He or she obviously idealizes *the opposite personality features or values.* The more your partner is unhappy with you, the more admonitions you receive from him, and the more stress liquid pours into his SA. You already know the consequences.

After you understand what kind of lessons you got from Life, you should make a decision. You may leave everything as it is—in which case your SA will continue filling. Or you may change your attitude to life, i.e., *stop idealizing things that are extremely precious to you on the subconscious level.* At the same time, consciously you are able to logically see that they do not have such a big importance to you. This approach can seem difficult, unless you stop idealizing.

Stop Idealizing

It is quite easy to do if we remember *the way of forgiveness.*

Forgive your spouse for what he or she does wrong, no matter how difficult it may be for you. You must realize that he only does things that you believe are mistaken to make you better, to teach you a lesson. Of course, he does it subconsciously because Life gave him this uneasy task.

As soon as you forgive your partner and accept him as he is, he will immediately change. He will have no need to teach you lessons anymore and will stop doing the things that bother you so much. Although he may still be doing something wrong, it will not bother you anymore because you will have already forgiven him.

At the same time, if your partner understands that you have a task to make him a better person, and he will forgive your spending too much time with friends, shopping, neglecting chores, drinking beer, or fishing, then you will no longer be obsessed with these activities.

You will still do them on occasion, yet without harming or offending your family.

Forgiveness alone is not enough, however; it is merely the *first stage* of correcting your destiny. We may forgive a person, but a day later we become offended or angry with him—again for the same reason. After you have comprehended what you value excessively, you should first forgive Life itself, your relatives, yourself, your bad luck, etc., and then *change yourself so that you no longer idealize much of earthly values.*

We will examine this kind of attitude in the third chapter. If this problem is your priority now, we urge you to proceed to the third chapter right away.

1.6   Common Lessons We Receive from Children

Children can also give spiritual lessons to their parents by. means of their character, habits, behavior, attitude toward life, etc.

It is especially difficult to deal on this account with the *first child* (when there are several children in the family).

Life may worry that the parents only intend to have one child, so its task is to have the first child teach them all of the necessary lessons. For this reason, the first-born child idealizes the opposite values of the parent who needs to be taught Life's lessons the most.

The first child destroys the values system of his parents. He usually possesses the following:

1. The qualities opposite to the ones idealized by his parents
2. The qualities that his parents despise in other people

These qualities will annoy his parents the most and will teach them the proper lessons.

Typical Ways to Destroy the Idealizations of the Parents Let us take a look at some of the common ways for children to destroy the idealizations of their parents:

1. A drug-addicted child may destroy his parents' love of discipline and sense of order, their devotion to moral norms, and their care about public opinion.
2. A child who does poorly at school destroys such values as knowledge, intelligence, planning and managing life, and public opinion.
3. A child who lives an alternative lifestyle (e.g., becomes a punk, rapper, etc.) will not allow his parents to idealize public opinion, rules of social behavior, or moral norms.
4. Some children show interest to sex quite early. This way, they destroy their parents' puritan views about sex, as well as their condemnation of sex and restrictions regarding intimacy.

5. A very spiritual child will not permit his parents to exaggerate the importance of material values.
6. A child who lies and steals will destroy the excessive honesty of his parents.
7. A child who is too independent will fight against the parental control over his life and against too much protection or care.
8. Children who are too attached to material values will struggle against extremely spiritual parents who condemn wealthy people.

As you know, difficult relationships that occur between parents and their children have always existed. Parents are always critical of new ideas and are attached to old ones.

Young people have the opposite perspective. Parents and their children give each other Life's proper lessons. This cycle will continue until the moment we learn to forgive each other and accept the views of the other party.

This system allows us to easily predict a child's character traits (especially those of the first-born). To determine a child's personality, we simply need to know the main idealizations of one of his parents.

Families with No Children

Now let us consider the situation when parents are unable to have children. What might be the reason?

The most possible explanation is that the parents idealize the idea of having a child and *cannot imagine life without children.* They live without a child for a long time and continuously experience stress and anxiety about not having children. They believe that their real life will only begin when they have a baby. This belief is mistaken. We live life right now, and we should learn to enjoy it the way it is given to us. That is why Life itself has to destroy the belief that a family cannot live without a child.

The situation may drastically change, however, if the parents reconsider their views and understand that their life is wonderful and full of happy events even without a child. Children simply make our lives fuller.

There may be another reason for an inability to have children. To correct the erroneous views of the parents, the child should possess a set of qualities that are in opposition to his parents' value system. The number of these qualities might be so big that a child would make his situation much worse in the process of making his parents better people. The child's SA would invariably become full. To avoid this result, the child's soul is not allowed into this world.

If the parents truly want to have a child, they should get rid of excessively important ideas about the world and their requirements and expectations regarding a future baby (its sex, talents, health, etc.). Instead, they should determine what exactly they idealize, reconsider their views, forgive each other, and accept our world as is. This way, *the mission of their future child will not be so complicated*, and he will be able to enter this world.

1.7 Common Lessons at Work

Most people spend half of their life at work (some of them even more). We call them "workaholics."

Work means a lot to us. It brings us material wellbeing and allows us to pursue our plans and dreams and gain power or prestige. For these reasons, there are many possibilities to start taking to your heart too much. As you understand, creating idealizations at work can result in spiritual lessons your Guardian will send your way.

The workplace contains many of the same objects of idealization that might be found in other situations.

Idealizing Material Values

While working, it is very easy to begin idealizing *money, material goods and expensive* things. It is very easy to become envious of your more successful coworker who has a better house or a car, without seeing big opportunities of changing your own financial situation.

Some people take it easy, while others plunge into a long-term grief on this account. If these things cause us to suffer, we start judging ourselves harshly, become unhappy with ourselves, or even take offense with Life for not providing us with enough money or material goods. We can also grow to be envious of other people who earn more.

These results do not mean that we should stop trying to earn more money or achieve material wealth. Earn as much as you can. Yet, developing the right *attitude toward material wealth is more important.* If you idealize material things and you if you believe that life without them makes no sense to you (if you exaggerate their significance), then you can face tremendous obstacles when you try to increase your income. This way, Life teaches you a lesson about your wrong attitude toward important material values— particularly, *you are living an acceptable life without these things, even if you do not believe that you have a decent life.*

This idealization takes different forms. Some of us hate wealthy people for being rich, and we believe that we are losers because we do not have as much money. Others passionately dream of buying a huge new house or a luxurious car, and they become depressed when these dreams do not come true. Yet, other people have the goal of earning a lot of money and become aggressive and hostile when they do not achieve the wealth that they idealize.

As you may have already guessed, it is absolutely normal to strive for a larger income, a better car, or a nicer house; however, we should not become offended or be annoyed with Life *for a long period of time* if things do not work out the way we want. We may turn upset and vent our frustration by swearing or hitting things to get rid of our negative emotions, but it is important that we do *not create prolonged negative emotions inside.* If these emotions start manifesting themselves, our Guardian will make an immediate effort *to make our life even worse. Now, when it got worse, we understand that it was really unwise to complain about our earlier material situation.* Life can always throw us down to the lower levels—to complete poverty, humiliation, or even death.

Idealizing Power

The other objects of idealization are *power, honor, worship, and excellence.* These values are usually idealized by individuals who own businesses, especially the ones who achieved tremendous success unpredictably fast. Let's say they were not very successful in the past and then suddenly jumped to being a head of a financial institution or a trade company, gaining almost unlimited resources and control over money, property, people, etc. For this reason, they *feel euphoria and they believe that they can do everything they want, becoming arrogant toward their less-fortunate colleagues.*

As you understand, such a person does not get to the upper levels.

Idealizing Trust in Other People

Another typical belief is an *excessive faith in people, exaggerating their honesty, decency, or responsibility.* This idealization may manifest itself in *too much trust in a business partner,* when you do not ask for proofs of reliability when doing business.

People often borrow money from each other, and it is normal; however, if you idealize the person to whom you lend the money, he will destroy your idealization by not paying you back.

Almost all of us have faced situations when our good acquaintances do not keep their promises. If you trust them too much and do not take measures to protect your interests, and they betray your trust, then all that is left for you is to grieve and become upset with Life. You should not get upset, however. You need to realize that *these events were meant to make you stop idealizing others,* placing too much trust in them.

Idealizing Our Plans

Another erroneous belief concerns the efforts to control the whole world and to achieve our goals at any cost. We all make plans for our future in one way or another; however, not all of us become unreasonably upset if our plans do not work out. When we are at work, it is easy for our Guardian to determine if we idealize our plans:

He simply destroys them. In these circumstances, the more we insist on sticking to our plan, the worse it will work out. If we cannot accept our failure as a loss in a game and we aggressively continue trying to achieve our goals at any cost, then we face even more counteraction from our Guardian.

We should not stop working toward our goals after a failure occurs. It is normal to make plans, pursue them, and apply our knowledge and energy toward achieving them.

Yet, we should *not take offense if something does not happen the way we want. Do not hold a grudge against those* people who do not meet your requirements, who disagree with you, or who do something incorrectly according to your point of view. *Do not judge them.* On the outside you may be strict, demanding, and even cruel, but only within the norms of the game called "my business."

You can get emotional, write complaints, and sue somebody, but do it without anger— with forgiveness, understanding, and compassion toward others when they lose.

If you do not pass Life's tests, get annoyed, and start judging others or yourself, then your situation will grow increasingly worse until your plans are completely destroyed by negative circumstances. This way, you will come to understand that it is not the end of the world when your plans fail.

The other extreme of this idealization manifests itself in an *excessive anxiety and doubt*: "Did I do everything correctly? What if something unexpected happens? Maybe I forgot something?" These kinds of questions indicate a lack of trust in your surrounding world and show

an *exaggeration of your inability to reach your goals.* This idealization will also be destroyed through unhappy events or illnesses brought to your life.

These principles apply to any kind of planning, whether it concerns a purchase, construction, education, or family planning.

Self-Diagnosis of the Spiritual Lessons While at Work

You can tell whether Life is trying to teach you any lessons when things stop working out for you.

If none of your plans are ever implemented and you consistently suffer misfortune, it means that Life is teaching you a serious lesson. Your SA is overflowing, and your problems might even worsen in the future. To help yourself, you must identify your idealizations and erroneous convictions, and ask Life to forgive you for *attaching too much importance* to your plans or other aspects of your life. You *exaggerate the importance of your goals*, but in reality, nothing frightening will happen to you if they never materialize. After all, you are alive and healthy, despite all your apprehensions and stress, and it seems that indulging yourself in suffering is the wrong thing to do.

Instead, you should deem *your problems as a loss of just one set in a game* and tune yourself to winning the next one; however, you should gear your anxiety to winning over yourself first of all, not over Life in general. *Life always wins*, no matter how things turn out.

To avoid having idealizations about work, it would be advantageous for you to *occasionally change jobs.* It will help you to detect early when you start to *attach excessive importance to your professional victories or defeats.* While keeping in mind that you will only have the same position at your present work for a limited number of years/months, you will not *attach excessive importance to your professional victories or defeats.* Thus, you will not be offended with Life, and it will be easier for you to become professionally successful.

It is not easy, however, for all of us to change our job or business. It is quite difficult for miners, railroad workers, pilots, farmers, etc. People of such professions should learn *not to take offense with their life*; otherwise, their idealizations will be destroyed severely. Sadly enough, our Guardians are not interested in our earthly problems. They want our souls to be perfect and are not concerned with how our bodies survive.

Of course, there are many other aspects of our earthly existence, such as business, private life, health, creative pursuits, hobbies, sex, and so on. We are constantly being taught lessons in each of these areas when Life uses the *same educational methods*: destroying our plans, wrecking our success, provoking spousal betrayal, etc.

For example, let us see how our idealizations can result in a car accident.

1.8 Common Lessons for Drivers

Only a few drivers are lucky enough to avoid car accidents.

There are many different reasons for these accidents, regardless of whose fault it is.

At first sight, all accidents have their own nature, except for one common thing—all of them are unexpected, except perhaps the cases involving drunk drivers.

Driving under the influence is considered being reckless, and it illustrates that a person idealizes his or her driving abilities.

This approach does not allow us to predict the accidents with a tragic outcome. We offer you another approach for foreseeing accidents, if you remember that everything in this world happens for a reason.

As you understand, *an accident is a way of destroying a driver's mistaken beliefs.*

Idealizing Your Abilities

We idealize our abilities if we prefer driving fast, passing other drivers by any means. This idealization manifests itself in *a feeling of superiority over other drivers and disdain for their driving.* Of course, we have similar attitude toward other people in other aspects of life, including work, but at the moment, we are considering only driving.

In reality, you have no reason for such judgment. No matter how fast and recklessly you drive, there is always someone who can be even more reckless.

You should not despise careful drivers either. You have no idea who drives other cars. It can be a priest, a college professor, or a world boxing champion who might have his own reasons to disdain you, and in case of a conflict, he will certainly be able to defend himself.

Your Guardian notices your false beliefs, and as soon as your SA becomes full, he starts teaching you lessons.

With the help of some adequate measures, he proves to you *that you do not drive so well after all.* At some point, he makes you absent-minded, and you become involved in an accident.

Life is merciful, so the lessons *gradually become stricter* according to the number of your negative thoughts and emotions you accumulate. Initially, fast drivers become involved in small accidents. If they do not learn the lesson, then harsher measures are applied. When the total number of negative convictions exceeds the norm, your physical life is taken away.

You may say, "So what? Does it mean I should not drive fast anymore?" Yes, you may drive fast! Yet, *you should not despise others for driving slower and more carefully than you do.* Change your values. Sympathize with other drivers, who are less able according to you. Apologize to them in your thoughts for your impatience and for your need to pass them on the road.

It does not seem to be a big deal; however, this attitude may save you a lot of time and money that you might otherwise need to spend on repairs and medical treatment.

Idealizing Your Car

Another common mistake is to *idealize material goods*—in this case, a vehicle. For some people, having a prestigious car as a possession becomes their main goal in life; it is stereotypical evidence of prosperity and happiness. This idealization leads to two kinds of erroneous beliefs.

If you have a very nice car, you might start to *feel superiority and contempt toward others* who have a despise others, developing an arrogant attitude. You allow yourself to despise others simply because they do not have such an impressive gadget as you do.

To help you get rid of this misconception, your Guardian may take measures to humble your arrogance and disdain for others by the means of making it more difficult for you to repair your car after an accident. It does not matter whether you or another driver is at fault. Your Guardians had agreed to involve the two of you in thisaccident to teach you both a lesson.

If you just go and repair your car without changing your attitude, the very object of your idealization may be taken away from you. Your Guardian may work it out with the Guardian of a thief who is destined to steal your car to deprive you of the original reason of your idealization— your car. So, it turns out that this very accident had been subconsciously provoked by your own attitude.

At the same time, you may experience difficulties acquiring a new automobile or when dealing with your insurance company, which may question the adequacy of your driving abilities. On the other hand, if you do not idealize your car, regardless of its splendor, nothing will happen to it. There is no reason for a future car thief to teach you any lessons.

The second idealization occurs when you have no car at all or if you are unhappy with the one you have and cannot afford to purchase a better one. You admire luxury cars and either secretly hate their owners or believe that you are unlucky in life. In his way, *you idealize wealth and material success* and condemn your present inadequate state.

To change your erroneous beliefs, your Guardian will take measures to worsen your financial situation, which compared to your previous one will seem quite a disaster.

Then you will understand that you should have appreciated your situation and should not have condemned Life.

It is a normal desire to have a luxurious car; *however, do not take offense with Life if something does not turn out the way you want* and if your financial situation is worse than that of other people, which does not allow you to buy a better vehicle.

If you think about it, you will realize that you are responsible for your poverty, but if you continue being discontented about your financial state, Life will keep teaching you lessons until you become very poor, get sick, or even die. For your Guardian, the purity of your soul is much more important than your obsession with material wealth.

Idealizing Discipline

Some of us *idealize discipline, order, and all sorts of rules.* It is commendable that we try to observe—let's say—the rules on the road; however, we sometimes attach excessive importance to these rules and aggressively condemn people who break them. We may expose our discontent by honking the horn, deliberately driving at a slow speed, or forcing others to pass us on the wrong lane. Alternatively, we may simply become angry inside without showing it.

In any case, our Guardian discerns this idealization and takes the necessary measures— namely, trying to mend our disposition concerning discipline. He will make us encounter a lot of lousy drivers who will force us to break all possible rules or get into an accident and hold us responsible for it.

Thus, he will continue teaching us until we stop being obsessed with order and discipline. This explanation does not mean that our Guardian dislikes discipline. He simply does not care much about the behavioral patterns established by people. Instead, our Guardian is concerned cleansing our soul and does not want us to become bitter or contemptuous.

Certainly, drivers are not the only ones with erroneous beliefs. Business people, politicians, scientists, artists, and other people have them, as well. We all belong to some professional environment and sometimes experience the peer pressure.

We showed you how to consider all of the events in our life from the following point of view: *If something happened, it means we received a lesson and must learn it.* We should determine what Life is teaching us and correct our mistakes.

Life is life, and we are not able to change it. We may only learn to understand its laws and try to follow them in our life.

Summary

1. Life constantly monitors our thoughts and actions. We permanently receive instructions within the norms of behavior that Life establishes.
2. We may do whatever we want; however, we should not attach excessive importance to any idea, event, person, or feeling.
3. Family life is one of the most effective areas where Life can destroy our idealizations. Couples who marry for love usually idealize different values. As a result, they teach each other lessons, and it becomes one of the primary reasons for family conflicts.
4. Children usually idealize values that are opposed to the values of one of their parents. This way, parents and children teach each other lessons and eradicate each other's idealizations.
5. Failures at work and an inability to fulfill our plans are good signs that we are being taught lessons by Life. In these situations, we need to change our attitude toward our goals and our other idealizations, and then these situations will improve.

1.9 Spiritual Lessons

In this chapter, we will explain to you how Life itself (with the help of our Guardian) heals our souls.

As you remember, the importance of our misconceptions may be determined by the level of the stress liquid in our Stress Accumulator. We also mentioned that our Guardian uses different ways to prove to us that our beliefs are false. Here are five ways Life can teach us.

1. *Direct Conflicts with Another Person Who Has an Opposing Value System*

This situation usually arises in families where the spouses have opposing values and are consequently functioning as "spiritual teachers" for each other without even knowing about it. If the parents idealize their children, then they will destroy their parents' convictions. Friends and business partners destroy each other's values systems, thus exchanging Life's lessons. Bosses teach subordinates, subordinates teach bosses, and so on.

2. *A Situation That Destroys Our Very Important Ideals*

There are situations when we cannot tell who exactly is teaching us a lesson. Most probably it is not only one, but several people subconsciously create circumstances that destroy our value system. For example, a person who idealizes money would lose it, and it is difficult to determine who provoked this result. He might work for a company that is going bankrupt, or his own business may collapse because of high taxes or unstable market. It is no one's fault.

So, why does Life take away money from the person who idealizes it? What is the purpose of such "healing"?

This way, we receive proof that we should *live in paradise every moment of our life* and that our discontent with Life results from our mistaken convictions. Let us see how Life proves it to us.

Let's assume that your income is $20,000 per year, and you are unhappy about it. It is difficult to be content when others earn $30,000 or more. Can you attain a bigger income?

Of course, you can. To achieve this goal, however, you should not take offense with your life and should instead seek real ways to increase your income. If you prefer to take offense and judge other people, Life will teach you a lesson, and your income will drop to only $10,000.

This income will still allow you to support yourself, but the previous one will now seem like a very decent income. If you do not regard this new situation as a lesson and do not apologize to Life for your criticism and taking offense, then Life will teach you again. Your $10,000 will be taken from you, and you will go on welfare or get disabled; instead of making money, you will become a burden to your relatives. Confined to bed, you will remember how good your life was when you had your health, were making $20,000, and had a strong opportunity to find a better- paying job. Compared to the present situation, it was almost a paradise. How could you be upset with life if you lived in paradise?

If, in your new and difficult situation, you recognize your misconceptions and apologize to Life, then Life will allow you to return to your life when you were healthy and making $20,000. If you are grateful to Life, you will earn much more, as long as you stay away from generating new idealizations.

Therefore, we receive instructions concerning money idealization, i.e., we are taught lessons when we are unhappy about our perceived lack of income. It is quite painful and unfair to us, but it is fair from our Guardian's point of view. People who idealize power, career, talents, control, and the like are taught in a similar manner. Life destroys their idealizations through situations that prove to them that they have the wrong attitude.

3. *Situations That Force Us to Do Things for Which We Criticize Others*

These circumstances arise when we judge others for their lack of common sense or discipline, frivolity, breaking norms of morale, etc.

Try to remember if you were ever upset with someone for being late for an important meeting or if you criticized another person for his unacceptable outfit.

Later, were you ever suddenly late for an important meeting or dressed improperly? It surely happened, but you never connected these events, especially because there may have been a certain gap in time between them. It may have seemed that these events happened due to a pure coincidence, but it is not true. These circumstances were *created especially for you to put you in the same situation in which the person that you judged had found himself before you.* You provoked your own situation to happen without realizing it.

If you faced a situation in which you had to compromise your own principles or standards and now you feel bad about it, *try to understand what caused this situation.* Try to recall who you recently judged for a similar behavior.

If you recall such an episode and ask for forgiveness in your thoughts, Life will not put you through the same test again. Yet, if you do fail to evoke the episodes that might have caused this situation, deem it as just a fluke, and continue to judge others, the situation might drag out for many years. You will always be late for important meetings and will become upset with yourself, or you will always dress improperly in important situations—or something similar will continue to cause you discomfort, providing you with reasons to judge yourself.

There is another and more unpleasant type of spiritual mentoring: *conflicts between parents and children.*

For example, your parents did not behave appropriately when you were young: They argued or fought with each other. It gave you a valid reason to be upset with them throughout your life. You assured yourself that such conflicts would *never happen in your family!* So when you grow older and create your own family,

Life will place you in the same situations as those of your parents (because you judged them). You may suddenly become irritable and start scandals for no apparent reason. Even if you try to keep your promise about not having arguments and scandals in your own family, you will allow others to provoke you. Your spouse will argue with you, your children will throw a tantrum, and your parents or other relatives will annoy you and provoke your hostility. This situation will continue until you stop reproaching your parents' early behavior. Then your Guardian will no longer have motivation to inflict such an unpleasant penalty onto your life.

4. *Situations That Implement Our Erroneous Beliefs on the Subconscious Level*

Imagine that you once borrowed money to invest it in your business, but your plan failed and you had a difficult time paying the money back. You finally met your financial obligations, but deep inside you are persuaded: "It is dangerous to start a private business" or "I am unable to be a successful businessperson."

Regardless of what you want and believe on the conscious level, your subconscious beliefs do not allow your business intentions to be carried out. You may get indignant or take enormous effort to proceed with your business, but nothing will seem to help. Your mistaken subconscious beliefs will cause events that bring you extra trouble.

If you are familiar with systems of achieving business success, then you know that one of the most important conditions for success in business is having *the right thoughts* and attitude. You should feel like a successful businessperson and look forward to your future achievements. It is quite difficult to feel this way if you have some hidden fears and apprehensions.

Subconscious fears and negative agenda can be developed in our mind concerning practically any issue. For example, having a negative experience being in love with a blonde girl earlier in your life will make you reluctant to develop the relationship with other blonde women for no apparent reason.

A mixture of fears and negative emotional patterns can inhabit our subconscious even when the original situation that triggered our fears is long forgotten. *It is only possible to determine that we have erroneous subconscious beliefs when we experience an emerging problem that has no other reasonable explanation. We also can detect these beliefs* when we analyze various complicated situations that occurred in our life and can define what conclusions or subconscious programs we encounter.

One of the sources of a negative subconscious programming is our own negative experience.

Parents Programming the Lives of Their Children

Another common source of negative programming is children's upbringing. Some parents are not afraid to be negative toward their kids, calling them "stupid," "clumsy," "lazy," etc.

Parental opinion is very important to children, so these words go straight to a child's subconscious and influence his or her whole life. As a result, even the most energetic child may grow into a very clumsy, stupid, or lazy adult, or he or she may feel this way.

In fact, very often *children experience a psychological attack from their parents.*

Parents attack children at the mental level, so it is extremely difficult to remove this negative program or change it at an older age.

We have met many people whose life was blemished by such subconscious negative programs, which made them skeptical and withdrawn. These personality traits do not allow a person to prosper in life.

There are more ways to show us how our subconscious can be negatively programmed and how it creates problems in our life.

5. *Situations That Take Us Out of the Usual Course of Events and Give Us Time to Reconsider Our Attitude Toward Life*

In these situations, Life usually makes us physically very ill in order to destroy our false beliefs, or it sends us to jail.

Our Guardian uses this kind of spiritual treatment when he cannot use the methods previously discussed—for example, when we judge ourselves or when we refuse or are unable to stamp out our own false beliefs.

These illnesses are meant to teach us a lesson, and if we have idealizations, then the illness is accompanied *by intense grief.* For example, if we idealize control over our relatives, we always watch over them and worry when they are on their own. Suddenly, we undergo an illness that does not allow us to move around very much, thus thinning our ability to watch over our relatives. In this manner, Life shows us that our relatives can live just fine without our guidance; however, we may resist learning this lesson, which will make it difficult to treat our illness with medications, and Life will not allow us to recover until we learn this necessary lesson.

In general, all means of spiritual treatment can be narrowed down to a simple principle:

Life gives us what we do not want and does not give us what we cannot imagine life without.

Correlation Between "Crime" and "Punishment"

The question remains: How soon will the Guardian give us penalty after we have formed our erroneous beliefs?

The answer to this question depends on the liquid level in our Stress Accumulator. If it is only 25–35% full, we will receive a lesson approximately 1–2 days after we start idealizing something.

If our SA is 70% or more full, we have been receiving instructions for a long time already and have simply not been paying attention.

This situation indicates that Life may not teach us another lesson in the immediate future.

If we did not understand the previous lessons, we will not understand the next one either. We will eventually receive our "punishment," but maybe a month, year, or even a decade later. Just keep in mind that, sooner or later, we will face problems unless we reconsider our life. When these difficulties occur will depend on how well we learn Life's lessons.

Summary

1. Life uses five ways to destroy our excessively important ideas and convictions.
2. Each of these ways is used according to the number of our mistaken beliefs and other negative circumstances.
3. The timing of Life's lessons depends on our ability to react to them, i.e., on the level of stress liquid in our Stress Accumulator.

2

Let's Get Rid of the Problems.

IN THIS CHAPTER, WE WILL CONTINUE TALKING ABOUT
Life's lessons and, more precisely, about the methods for getting
rid of the "educational" measures taken by the surrounding
world against us.

Getting Rid of All Problems

What should we do in order not to be taught by Life? In general, *we
should get rid of the negative stress that we already have and should
not accumulate any new stress.* Yes, it is not that easy. We might have
accumulated negative emotions for many years, so simply saying
"I forgive everybody," even sincerely, will hardly help us to get rid
of all the accumulated negative stress.

Also, it is hard to stop stressing out right away only by figuring
out what our idealizations are; we need more help here. That is
why we are ready to offer you valuable recommendations to ease.
up the transition to your new life without stress.

In this book we are going to use an esoteric model of the man,
which not only considers a human being as a material object
(physical body), but also illustrates that a human being possesses
a spiritual (subtle material) component called either aura or soul
(in religion).

According to this model, a human being consists of a physical body and six subtle non- material bodies.

Therefore, we keep in mind that a human being presents a very complicated structure consisting of the physical body, as well as non-material ones such as energy, emotional (astral), mental, and several other subtle bodies.

Together, they form what is called the "immortal soul" that moves from body to body in the process of reincarnation.

The materialists who do not believe in the existence of subtle bodies might instead think of the different psyche components, i.e., health (energy), emotions, and thoughts (mental body).

Our experience shows that all subtle bodies influence our life. Our immortal soul may also bring from the past some problems that we are unaware of. That is why we should look deeper into our soul.

So if you are going to become a "saint"—that is, clean your Stress Accumulator (SA) —we suggest you purify all your subtle bodies. Otherwise, the cleansing or treatment will not be efficient, or the results will only be temporary.

What Are We Going to Clean?

Is it a good idea to get rid of every single problem in our life? This question is not that simple to answer. It is easy to come to a conclusion that total cleansing may result in losing interest in life.

We already mentioned earlier that only saints have an empty SA, as *they have no desires in this world.* If we successfully clean our SA, the same will happen to us.

Everything will be possible for us, but we will not want it.

Nothing will worry us, as we will calmly accept anything that Life brings.

Would you like to face such a future? We guess not.

More precisely, such a goal is virtually impossible to achieve. We all want to lead an active life, buy nice things, and feel *alive*, even if it involves having to pay bills or arguing with relatives or friends. Life does not allow us to be entirely tranquil and remote, and we can never avoid temptations. So what can we do?

We suggest you choose problems you want to get rid of i.e., you should select several valves of the SA that are the most important for you. Let some stress liquid in through these valves, i.e., you may still slightly idealize some aspects of life (love, family, money, art, etc.); however, try to keep the other valves closed by staying away from condemning, judging, or despising other people.

Then you will be able to live your life joyfully, and your SA will only be 45–55% full. As we already mentioned, this percentage represents the best situation for allowing all of your earthly dreams to come true.

If this recommendation sounds good to you, let us tell you what methods and techniques will help you transform into this comfortable state. Even if you want to become a "saint" and are not interested in earthly values, our method will help you. Using it is not enough to become a saint, however; for this, you need other, more complicated techniques. But that's a different story. Now let us talk about cleaning our SA.

2.1   Say Goodbye to Your Negative Emotions!

Everything in this world is ruled by emotions. So let us start with learning some techniques that will help you to cleanse your subtle body. *This body stores all our offense, condemnation, memories of jealousy or anger, and other positive or negative emotions.* If the emotions were positive, then memories of them make our life more pleasant, and as a result, we will not fight them.

Negative emotions have a different effect. Almost all of us have been feeling such emotions from our childhood, and we probably feel them now. We already mentioned where these emotions come from. Our mind idealizes the world, but the real world is dramatically different from our model. Having noticed this difference, you may stop paying attention to it or may try to change the world according to your ideas, if it is possible. You may also do nothing and feel a great deal of negative stress, wondering why everything goes so wrong.

Emotions Are Stored as Thought-Forms.

Each stressful emotion is accompanied by a certain set of thoughts. As a result, each strong emotion forms a corresponding *thought-form* (bundle of energy and information) that is stored in our emotional body in the form of a dirty stain (in case of a negative emotion). In other words, all stress is recorded in the cell memory of our body. The stronger our offense or condemnation is, the larger and denser the corresponding thought-form is.

Thus, unfortunately, our stress does not disappear. It is *stored in the emotional body* and initiates the stress outbursts in our uncontrollable mind. So when we see a person looking even a little like our offender, our memory produces a corresponding thought-form, and we start thinking of all our offenses and go through them again. In this way, the existing thought-form becomes more dense and massive. As you understand right now, this is how our SA gets filled.

All Offenses Stay Inside Us.

By the moment we turn, say, forty, we might possess a lot of negative thought-forms. Each of them is connected with some person—your father, mother, children, husband or wife, boss, or any other people who cause us negative stress.

Sooner or later, the stress weakens, and it seems as if we do not take offense and do not condemn anymore. At least we believe so, as we have already forgotten the negative events and the accompanying stress. Sadly, the reality is different. We might have forgotten the negative stress that we experienced in our childhood, but this stress still stays in our emotional body and we need to activate certain procedures to get rid of it.

More precisely, the negative thought-forms do somehow melt away, but very slowly, especially if we accumulated them with years by taking offense with someone or condemning people. After so many years, the thought-forms became large and dense, and *we cannot eliminate them simply by forgetting about our offender.* Nor can we get rid of them by consciously forgiving the offenders.

It is true that forgiveness will block a corresponding valve of the SA, but the stress liquid level will hardly change.

As our offenses and condemnations are stored in our subtle bodies, our Guardian will have to use the third way of destroying our idealizations, i.e. he will *put us in the situation of the person whom we condemned.*

We already gave you an example of typical lessons for the family.

Let's say a child condemns his parents for the discord in their relationship. Therefore, a large thought-form concerning the condemnation of his parents gets stored in his emotional body.

When the child grows older, he may consciously forgive his parents and change his attitude toward them (especially if one of them dies). The thought-form of offence or condemnation does not go away, however; it is still with him. Our Guardian is aware of it, so he has to apply "educational" measures to this person i.e., to create the same situation that annoyed him concerning his parents.

Let Us Erase Negative Thought-Forms.

To avoid such "educational" measures, we need to find a way to *erase these thought- forms in our emotional body.* Who is able to do it best? Ourselves, of course, because it is our own problem. We need a special tool for this cleansing, something that can interact with the subtle matter of our emotional body.

There exist many tools for this purpose—for instant, seeing your psychotherapist is not such a bad idea, as well.

Yet, such a specialist usually works with *one very strong emotion ruining your life* that made you ask for help (offense taken with a girlfriend who left you or a husband who dumped you for another woman, etc.). We need to deal with all of the thought-forms that are responsible for our stress, however, including the ones we forgot all about a long time ago.

Let Us Totally Clean the Emotional Body.

That is why we suggest you totally cleanse your emotional body and get rid of any negative thought-forms that appeared due to interaction with other people. During lifetime, you meet many people, so while cleaning your emotional body, you should take *them all* into account.

If you are a young person and have never been very tactful, then you might possess hundreds of negative thought-forms, depending on the number of people who caused you negative stress. You emotional body is very dirty, and it will take an effort to clean it.

Remember All Your Acquaintances.

We recommend that you *make a list of all the people* you interacted with in your early childhood, at school, in college, at work, at home, etc. Try to remember details and put every person on this list.

The first entries of your list should represent people about whom you *felt the most negative emotions.* Then list all the others. You will have to clean your emotional body, *thinking separately about each of these people.* It is not easy and will take one to two months of work.

"Cleaning" Takes a Long Time.

If you try to forgive your enemies all at once and feel love toward them, you will still not stop receiving spiritual "lessons" from your Guardian. Feeling love toward your enemies will just result *in closing the valves* through which negative emotions enter your the SA. It will mean that your SA stops filling, but the stress liquid level will remain the same for some time.

That is why changes for the better often do not happen immediately, even when you "start loving everybody." Things may even become worse. It is very sad, is it not? What can you do in this situation?

One of the lower pipes of the SA is called "Conscious Actions." To quickly clean your SA, you should use its capacity, i.e., *take conscious actions to clean your SA.* Being merciful and charitable will do, but it is a slow path. To have this pipe release your sins quickly, you need to do certain exercises.

One of the exercises we recommend is called Meditation of Forgiveness. It is a well-known exercise used in various spiritual schools in one form or another.

This exercise will also help you to *stop the train of negative thoughts. It is based on the well-known principle of replacing uncontrolled thoughts* by positive ones.

You may do the exercise at any time. For example, when walking down the street, riding a bus, attending a meeting, waiting for someone, etc.

Meditation of Forgiveness Exercise

Choose a person you got offended by (or you feel a negative emotion toward). You need to erase your thought-form concerning this person. In our example, let it be a husband.

Start repeating this phrase for a long time: "With love and gratitude, I forgive my husband and accept him as he was created by God *[or, as he is]*. I ask my husband for forgiveness for my thoughts and emotions toward him."

Repeat this phrase until you feel warmth in your heart.

This sensation indicates that the negative thought-form concerning this person is completely erased.

Some very emotional people reach this sensation within five minutes. Other people never feel this warmth, and that is fine, too. To achieve successful results, you need to spend a certain amount of time on this meditation.

If you had tense relationship with someone for many years, then you need to spend three to five hours on this meditation.

This time may consist of short meditations that you can do in your free time. If you did not have serious conflicts with this person, then you need to spend thirty to fifty minutes on the meditation.

After you get rid of the thought-form, start repeating the following phrase in your mind: "With love and gratitude my husband forgives me." *In this way, you will erase a negative thought- form that was* "given" *to you by your husband during your conflicts.*

Repeat this phrase until you feel warmth in your chest again or you see your husband inside your mind. If his negative thought-form is successfully erased, then your husband may turn his face to you, smile, or even wave his hand (in your mind, of course). It means that your emotional body was cleansed of all offenses and other negative emotions.

Apply This Principle to Everyone You Know.

We only considered the meditation of forgiveness concerning a husband. Yet, it is only the first step toward cleaning your emotional body.

Next, you need to do the same thing concerning your *father, mother, siblings, exhusbands, or wives*, if you had tense or conflicting relationship with them.

Then meditate about *all your relatives (each one separately)* who interacted with you and caused you trouble.

Do not forget *the acquaintances at work* or the people you practice your hobbies with, unfair bosses or ungrateful subordinates, *your loved ones with whom you parted, and last, but not least, yourself* if you get angry with yourself. The phrase to use here is almost the same: "I ask myself for forgiveness for my thoughts and emotions concerning myself. With love and gratitude, I forgive myself and accept myself as I am."

People tend to judge themselves. (Why am I so unlucky, ugly, shy, or stupid?) They take offense with themselves and feel guilty all the time; however, *self-condemnation is a sin as serious as condemnation of other people.*

That is why it is necessary for us to forgive ourselves.

Next, you should pay attention to *Life in general.* Most likely, you sometimes took offense with Life for taking away your loved one or your relative, or for making your life too difficult.

The phrase for this meditation is the following: "With love and gratitude, I forgive Life and accept it as it is. I ask Life for forgiveness for all negative thoughts and emotions toward it. With love and gratitude, Life forgives me."

The ultimate meditation time depends on how deeply you are upset with Life. The meditation concerning people with whom you had the most conflicting relationship will require *several hours of meditation.* For old acquaintances or relatives who you can hardly remember, you should work ten to thirty minutes (for each).

Try to determine yourself how much time you will need for this exercise. A person over forty years old will need at least a month of work to completely get rid of all offenses. The general meditation time should not be less than thirty hours.

While reading this chapter, you might think: Why should I repeat the forgiveness meditation for such a long time? It seems like you no longer remember the offense that you took with some people, forgave some, and already feel compassion toward other ones. Your mental level is clean. Then why do you keep "getting lessons" from your Guardian?

Sins as Dirty Stains on Paper

To answer this question, let us use a simple comparison.

Imagine that your negative thought-form is a dirty stain on a sheet of paper. The larger and darker the thoughtform, the bigger the stain appears.

You need to clean the paper, but the eraser that you have is really small. Every move of the eraser cleans a small part of the dirty surface. To clean the entire sheet, we need to perform a lot of cleaning movements. The bigger the stain, the more moves we use.

That is why we suggest you repeat the forgiveness meditation in your mind many times. Each repetition erases only a small part of your thought-form. If you realize that your former beliefs were incorrect and forgive your enemies, you erase a big part of your thought-form; however, you only erase a bit at a time.

Therefore, while forgiving and accepting the world, *do not forget about your former offenses and indignation.* Work with them separately, and your Guardian will not have to apply "educational" measures to you anymore.

Summary

1. All the negative stress that we feel is stored in our emotional body as thought-forms (dark bundles of thoughts and emotions).

2. Negative thought-forms do not get erased immediately after we change our attitude toward the world and forgive our former enemies.

3. To quicken the process of cleansing the emotional body, we suggest practicing the Forgiveness Meditation, i.e., erasing a negative thought-from by repeating a certain phrase.

4. The Forgiveness Meditation should be applied to all people with whom we had tense relations, including relatives, acquaintances, Life, and ourselves.

2.2 Changing your views

The forgiveness meditation allows us to get rid of our former stress and eliminate the consequences of new ones coming into your life. Yet, if we do not change anything about our thoughts, we will always have to forgive others.

We will always become involved in scandals and conflicts first, and then we'll have to do the process of forgiving.

If we want to live more consciously, we should learn not to store new stress, i.e., block the valves (idealizations).

This will only happen when we stop attaching excessive importance to our expectations, i.e., we get rid of our idealizations.

At the same time, we need to start working with our mental level because it stores all of our ideas, knowledge, and information about our experiences and the idealizations created by our mind. As you may remember, idealizations are the source of our discontent with life, filling the SA and causing us to receive "lessons." As a result, *we urgently need to get rid of our erroneous beliefs and idealizations stored at the mental level.*

You Live in Paradise!

There exists an idea that can help us in life every time we suffer stress. It seems very simple, although not all people understand and accept it easily. Here it is: *You should accept that you live every single moment of your life in Paradise!* It is true for every single moment, no matter how terrible it may seem to you!

It is difficult to assume such an attitude toward life.

Life teaches us "lessons" all the time, and that is why we do not feel like we are in Paradise.

Could your life become even worse? You probably have never thought about it because all methods (including our Method of Forming Events) encourage you to think positively. You try hard to think positively, but life only gets worse.

It is clear why life continues to worsen. We are unhappy with it, our SA fills, and Life takes increasingly strict "educational" measures. Yet, these measures are not *a punishment or revenge*; they just help changing our erroneous beliefs!

If we dream about a better life and keep being discontent about our present state, the *situation is likely to grow worse.* That is why we suggest you do not dig your head in the sand like an ostrich in case of danger, but try to look at your *possible unhappy future from the point of view that it could be even worse.*

It is easy to just imagine how much worse Life may turn. It only *depends on what area of life you are unhappy with.* If you are upset with your family life, the situation in this area could always be worse. Yet, if your work situation is not very important for you, things in this field will still be okay, and you will be able to earn your living.

And vice versa.

What can we do to avoid worsening the situation after we have determined our idealizations? How do we get rid of them when we like them so much?

It is simple. We just need to understand that *right now we live in Paradise.* If we do not admit it now, one day we will find ourselves in Hell. Then life will grow much worse. Of course, Paradise and Hell are very conditional notions. It is difficult to accept that we live in Paradise when the money we earn is hardly enough to pay our bills and all attempts to change the situation lead to nothing.

It is not Hell either, but a lack of money stains our life as much as being homeless stains the life of a poor person who does not have a place to live.

If you are unhappy with your life for a long time, it means that you have explicit idealizations. As a result, Life just *has* to prove that you live in Paradise, not in Hell, as you think.

How can Life do it? We already mentioned that "educational" measures are applied to the area of life you are unhappy with.

Let's say, now you are upset about your financial situation, so

Life will take money from you. It is hard to tell how it will happen because Life has many opportunities for achieving its goals.

For example, you will get a new boss who will dislike you for some reason and will try to demote you or even fire you, which will result in job loss and, possibly, poverty.

Or there will be less demand for the products of your company, so the administration will lay off some personnel, including you. Or something else resulting in the loss of income will occur.

It will not make you more optimistic, and the new situation will seem like Hell to you.

Finding yourself in this new situation, you will interpret your life a year ago as being happy. Your income was not great, but at least stable. In this way, Life proves to you how wrong your views are. Your present life sounds like Paradise compared to a life of a jobless person, and you have to admit it.

Of course, compared to the life of a rich man, your life does not seem that happy. Yet, you have an opportunity to increase your income if *at any moment* you are ready to admit that you live in Paradise. Do not condemn Life, but ask it to give you a well-paying job or your own business.

There are plenty of possibilities in this world, so if you ask in a right way, you will surely receive what you want. Yet, if you do not get it, think which of your beliefs hinders you from achieving the goal that millions of other people have already achieved.

This approach *(admitting that any moment of your life you live in Paradise)* may help you close all SA valves and cleanse your mental body.

We probably need a *more practical approach*, such as particular breathing or some physical exercise. *These practical tools* are easy to grasp, but sadly, they will not help us much get rid of our mistaken beliefs. The reason is that our mental body generated these beliefs, and we cannot change our mental body through physical efforts because it is not directly connected with our physical body.

Tools for Changing Our Erroneous Beliefs

Consequently, we need to find some tools to change our attitude toward life and our beliefs. Do these tools exist at all? Yes they do. One of them is self-programming (i.e., *using positive statements or affirmations*).

Affirmations

These techniques are meant to replace our erroneous beliefs by *positive thoughts*. It is a good technique, but *it requires a major effort to "reprogram"* our mistaken convictions.

For years, our troubled mind has been filling our mental level with idealizations and erroneous beliefs.

Therefore, to get rid of them as soon as possible, we need *to intensely fill ourselves with positive assertions*. The total amount of positive thoughts should be *at least equal to* the number of negative ones. We do not have many years to replace our beliefs, so *reprogramming should be really intense*.

This goal is easy to achieve at group classes with a good mentor who creates a high-energy environment and who allows people to feel euphoria and excitement. After two or three seminars, instead of condemnation, we will feel love toward others and ourselves.

Yet, if you try to use this method at home by using a book, achieving results will take longer. It is quite difficult to reach a state of euphoria when your mind is filled with problems and doubts. Some people manage to do it well, so affirmations work quickly and efficiently. People who want to think positively but cannot get rid of constant doubts, however, face a problem and can do very little about it. Those people may use another, purely mental tool to fight their wrong convictions.

Don't Create Your Unhappy Future!

This method is very simple and originates from a simple idea: Let us not wait for Life to use all "educational" measures against us. We should *get ahead and only* imagine *what measures may be applied to us.* It is easy to do while using a simple exercise called the Pincushion of Events.

Don't create your unhappy future!

This method is very simple and is based on a simple idea: Let's not wait for life to use all the "educational" measures against us. We need to get ahead of events and only imagine what measures can be applied to us. This is easy to do with a simple exercise called "**The Hedgehog of Events**".

Let's see how it works when you are certain that things have to be the way you want them to be and can't imagine that life could go any other way.

For example, your father was a kind, tactful and well-mannered man, and you can't imagine him any different (i.e. you idealize relationships between people).

Now that he is older, he may exhibit negative character traits (rudeness, irritability, etc.). The more you judge him for this behavior, the worse it will get (only towards you). His relationships with other people may be bad or good.

However, his attitude toward you will get worse and worse until you change your attitude toward him.

Do you think your father is the worst father in the world? If you think about it, you will probably realize that he is not. You can always find a worse person.

So if you don't want your father to get worse, imagine that he's already gotten much worse. Then the problems you are experiencing with him now will seem like only a small part of what could have happened. He could have gotten worse, but he didn't! Look how good he is! Why did you condemn him?

And yet he could change for the worse if you don't change your attitude towards him, that is, now he makes you think you are living in paradise, but soon life may show you hell.

This principle will help you more easily survive any situation, no matter how bad it may seem at first glance.

The exercise we offer you is based on this principle.

Exercise "Hedgehog of Events"

Ask people not to bother you for fifteen to twenty minutes.

Take a comfortable position, close your eyes, relax your body and try to stop the flow of your thoughts.

Imagine that your life can take several different turns, so that all the events in your life are represented as a set of needles (each needle represents an event) in a Hedgehog (Fig. 2).

Of all the possible events, you would like only one to happen, the one that suits you best (one needle). In reality, by destroying your idealizations, Life causes worse and worse events to happen to you (the second needle, etc.).

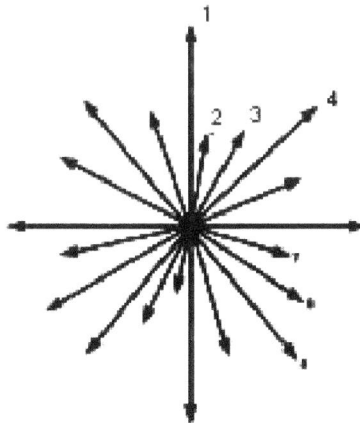

Imagine what may happen to you if Life continues applying "educational" measures to you, i.e., conditions of your life keep worsening (more pins).

Imagine (e.g., for five to ten minutes) that you live through each possible negative event. Imagine what you will do, how you will interact with others and the world, and what your thoughts will be.

After living through each event, say to yourself: "Life! If you find it necessary to change my life to this extent, I will accept it without doubts and offense. There must be some reason why you are giving me this lesson. If I really need this lesson, then I accept it with gratitude."

In the same manner, you should "live" through events that gradually become worse. The rest of the pins represent them.

After each exercise, confirm that you will accept any lesson without anger and condemnation, but ask Life not to apply these measures to you.

At the end, confirm again that you do not condemn the present situation, that you consider it as a lesson that you deserved for your thoughts and actions, and that this situation is the best of all. You are grateful for the lesson you have received, accept you present situation as a very good one, and ask Life to possibly make it better, i.e., the way you want.

By performing this exercise, you avoid "programming" of a negative future by asking Life *not to apply measures to you*. At the same time, you let Life know that you accept everything that happens not as a punishment or revenge, but as a lesson taught to you for your erroneous thoughts or behavior.

Let us take as an example that involves the same father we mentioned before.

First (the most desired) pin represents normal, quiet relationship between you two.

The second pin represents the existing situation when he is rude to you and provokes conflicts.

The third pin *may represent the situation when your Dad gets sick and you have to take care of him*. His character will not change for the better.

The fourth pin, he starts drinking and brings his drinking friends over. The fifth pin, he brings loose, drunk women home. The sixth pin, he treats his grandchildren badly. The seventh pin, he accidentally sets the house on fire being drunk. The eighth pin, he starts selling valuable things from the house.

There exist a vast variety of events (pins). *You should pretend living through all of them without taking offense with Life* (fortunately, not in reality, but only in your imagination).

Imagine what happens when the third, fourth, and following events will take place—all possible relationships, patterns, money situations, etc.

Then say to yourself: "Life, if I deserve it, I will accept this situation and will not complain because I understand that this situation is the result of my negative emotions toward my father. Yet if it is possible, let my dad stop spoiling our lives."

This mental exercise will help you get ahead of *"educational" measures* and prove to Life that you are aware of possible future lessons *and are ready to accept them*, and that you consider the existing situation as a very good one and realize that, due to your discontent, it may get even worse. Yet, you are not discontent with the present state anymore, so Life does not have to apply stricter measures to you. If your life is good now, it will only get better in the future.

We recommend that you use this technique to destroy any idealizations that you may have, as well as to get rid of your discontent about life. It is easier to be glad about the present than anticipate the problems that the future may/may not bring.

Could Things Get Worse?

To anticipate possible questions, let us tell you right away that this exercise *does not program a negative future* because, in the end of each event analysis, we add the following phrase: "Life, if it happens, I will accept it without any complaints and anger. Yet, if it is possible, let events happen the way that I want them to (express here an event you want to happen)."

In this way, you let Life know *that you do not need negative events*. You are prepared for them, but you do not need them. You need other things that have not happened yet, but you are not stressed out about them anymore because you understand that your Life is happy anyway.

Consequently, you do not demand anything from Life but express politely your request, which lowers your pride and arrogance. Life appreciates people who are not too proud and arrogant, and helps them if they ask for help.

Do Not Turn Your Life into a Pincushion of Events.

Let us give you one more recommendation. The "pincushion" exercise is a *one-time tool* to help you feel that your problem is not that serious after all, and to change your attitude toward events that you consider terrible. You should play with your "terrible situation" for ten to twenty minutes, and then realize that in reality everything goes well. Then go and enjoy your life.

Imagining negative events all day long will not do you any good. Your mind might start programming problems that you think about a lot. It may even lead to depression.

So stop the train of negative thoughts with the help of this method and start enjoying life! Do not use the Pincushion of Events exercise more often than once a week for ten minutes. Good luck to you!

When Can We Use This Method?

You may always use this exercise when it seems to you that your current situation cannot get any worse. The method will help you to quickly change your attitude toward the situation and bring down your stress.

For example, imagine that your child spends too much time at the computer. Do you constantly stress out about it? Perform the Pincushion of Events exercise and realize how good it is that he stays home and does not hang out with bad boys down the street.

Perhaps your husband drinks a pack of beer every day.

Do you worry that he is turning into a heavy drinker? Do the exercise and realize how good it is that he only drinks one pack and that it is just beer.

Maybe your wife talks on the phone a lot, and it annoys you a great deal. After the exercise, you will realize how good it is that you know all her friends, what they do, and what interests your wife, so you can feel that you can control your family life better.

Summary

1. To get rid of your discontent with life, you should accept that you live in Paradise every moment of your Life.
2. To avoid worsening the situation, you may get ahead of a problem. Try to live through possible worsening events. At the end of this exercise, tell Life that you are ready to accept any situation without discontent and condemnation. Yet, ask Life to improve your existing situation, if possible.
3. The Pincushion of Events exercise is meant to make you imagine aggravating life events to prove to you that your life at present is much better than you think.

3

How to Remain a Favorite of Life

WE ALREADY KNOW THE REASON WHY LIFE teaches us lessons. We also imagine how to avoid its educational measures.

Now if we reached a joyful state of mind, we should learn not to lose what we have accomplished. It is easy to lose what we have achieved because we have not yet experienced any radical changes. Also, people around us might be jealous of how much we smile and how little we suffer from stress. They do not understand us anymore, and even find us cold, as we suddenly became more balanced.

People may start accusing us of indifference, heartlessness, etc. We should be prepared for this treatment. Let people think of us whatever they want, and let us not try to answer their expectations; otherwise, we will have a new reason for stress, and new "educational measures" will follow.

How do you avoid stress when people and circumstances provoke you to it? You know that serious stress is harmful to you, but there is no chance for you to perform the Forgiveness Meditation all the time. You already used some forgiveness techniques, and your Stress Accumulator is not very full anymore. You do not want it to overflow again. You want to remain a favorite child of Life. How do you reach this goal?

To remain one of Life's favorites, we suggest that you choose and assume a certain attitude that will allow you to be in a good mood under any circumstances and to stop reacting emotionally, i.e., stop having a negative reaction.

Instead, you should react positively, i.e., smile, laugh at yourself, and tease others in a kind way. In these ways, you will be able to block the Valves (idealizations) and continue emptying your SA, which will lead you to happiness.

In this chapter, we will consider several attitudes that will help you properly arrange your life and achieve your desired goals.

1.1 Life Is a Circus.

Adopting the attitude that "life is a circus" helps us apply our sense of humor to any situation that we previously considered terrible. According to this attitude, we consider all people to be "clowns" in the "circus of life."

The more we suffer from stress, the better we play our role in this circus. Are you not yet tired of being a clown?

There is a famous statement: "Life is a theatre." We agree with this view but are intentionally trying to make an even stronger claim. For many people, becoming a theatrical actor may seem an attractive idea. What about becoming a clown in the circus? Our life is not a theatre at all. It is a real circus where *we all play the role of clowns.*

Yet, we do not understand it and take offense.

Life Is a Performance in the Arena.

To assume the attitude that «life is a circus», we should accept that e*verything happening in life is a performance at the circus arena.* People are clowns, and each of them has their own performance. The more emotional a person is in his/her everyday life, the more he/she takes offense and participates in conflicts, becomes angry, and preaches to others, and the better their role.

The Spectator Role

In this way, we spend all our life at the arena. Until now, you have been an active participant of this performance.

Now we suggest that you *leave the arena, sit in the audience, and watch the performance without participating in it.* You may laugh or be compassionate, but do not participate.

It is necessary to participate in a certain performance (e.g., love, career, etc.), you may return to the arena and take an active part in the performance to achieve your goals. Play the game called "life is a game" (which we will discuss later). When you have achieved your goals, return to the audience.

It is crucial for us to realize that, *if we are discontented about something, argue with someone, or condemn other people, we again become clowns and participate in the performance*, while wearing a funny hat with the name of our role on it.

There are a great variety of roles that we may play in the circus of life, including the following:

- *Life Mentor, Domestic Tyrant, Control Freak*—for people who like to tutor their families and interfere with their lives
- *Martyr*—for those who enjoy telling others about their suffering
- *Smart Alec*—for people who idealize their abilities and despise others, considering them "stupid"
- *Altruist*—for those who do everything for others, but who have no time for themselves
- *Sex addict*— who thinks and talks about sex all the time
- *Victim of a Lazy Employee*—for a boss suffering from great stress and whose subordinates do not perform their duties well enough
- Victim of Freaky Parents—*for people who suffer from excessive parental control*

These roles are just some common examples. You may invent your own funny hat to poke fun at your stress.

The funnier and more cynical the role you play in the circus of life, the easier it will be for you to get rid of it. By the way, make sure you design your own funny hat and not use the hats for other people!

While inventing your role, step away from your stress and look at it from afar. From this vantage point, you will discover that all the stress is ridiculous; everything that seemed terrible will seem funny.

You will start smiling, Life will come to your aid, and your situation will be easily resolved. Life likes smiling on people and is always ready to help them. Conversely, if you behave like you have terrible problems, Life will treat you accordingly.

It is amazing how most people fervently play their role in the circus of life *without having any real-life goals!* Life for many people consists solely of participating in the circus performance. These people cannot even imagine that it is possible to lead a different life without senseless fighting for nonexistent goals. Let us try to make our lives different!

Being in the Audience

Being *a spectator does not mean that you should just contemplate and do nothing.* You should observe all necessary rules of behavior—go to work, make work plans and fulfill them, prepare documents, hold negotiations, argue with suppliers or partners, make a declaration of love, etc.

Yet, youshould do all these things without being emotionally involved in these events, as if you were just a spectator. This attitude will keep you from becoming extremely attached to anything and, therefore, not add new stress to your SA.

Let us give you an example of such behavior. Imagine that you are the boss of a small department. You have a deadline for purchasing certain goods for your customer.

Suddenly, you realize that due to unfavorable circumstances, you cannot complete this task in time. For example, the necessary goods will only be produced within a month, while all existing goods have been already sold.

In this situation, it is easy for you to determine if you are at the arena or in the auditorium. If you suffer stress, argue, or complain to others about your problems, it means that you are at the arena. Stressing out and crying will not really help to improve your situation. In any case, you have to wait and consider this situation as inevitable.

You must quietly wait for the necessary events to , while keeping an eye on the rest of your life. Otherwise, you will suffer stress, argue, and take anti-anxiety medication while you are waiting, and therefore play an active role in the circus performance.

Sometimes We Must Side with Others.

Sometimes we have to participate in the performance despite our reluctance. Otherwise, we may face some unwanted problems.

Let us give you an example of such situation. Natalia works for a small company. All her coworkers are women, but her boss is a man. He is not very good at his work and makes many mistakes, but the senior executives prefer not to notice. They are also men, so it is easier for them to communicate with a person of the same gender.

Women in this firm mostly gossip about the boss and condemn his actions. Natalia used to participate in this "performance" and feel stressed out, and as result she faced "educational measures" from Life.

After reading our books and participating in our training events, Natalia was no longer interested in gossiping and stopped participating in the "performance."

As a result, she became a "black sheep." Coworkers started avoiding her and even insisted on having her fired. The clowns did not like her new attitude and started considering her a new enemy.

Despite these circumstances, Natalia really enjoyed her job and did not want to leave. As a result, she had to return to the circle of clowns and again condemn the boss as her coworkers did. Yet, in this situation, she was just playing the role of a "clown" without really condemning her boss and collecting new stress. Instead, she was making fun of her new role. It seemed like she rejoined the group, and consequently, her coworkers stopped being her enemies. As you can see, becoming a spectator led Natalia to certain problems that she managed to resolve without much additional stress.

How This Attitude Differs from Total Denial

We would like to emphasize that *the "life is a circus" attitude is not the same as going into denial,* which is sometimes recommended by psychologists in cases of complicated life situations.

Many people just stop reacting to any offenses and insults.

It happens in families in which one spouse assumes all of the power and dictates to the other spouse how to live. Sometimes it may even sound insulting, so the other spouse may react accordingly.

These situations most likely lead to a conflict.

Sometimes, however, the other spouse starts drinking or goes *into a deep denial,* i.e., stops reacting to any complaints or insults. This attitude seems similar to the "life is a circus" attitude, but it is not actually the same.

In this situation, *it is very important to know what really goes on inside a person's soul.* If he or she honestly manages to *isolate himself or herself without emotionally reacting to complaints and attacks,* and instead makes fun of the situation, then everything continues just fine. The person is not offended with Life, and as a result, his/her SA does not become filled.

Yet, more often, things work out differently.

Sometimes the powerful spouse is able to find new buttons to push, which leads to emotional outbursts from the significant other. As you might have guessed, the level of the stress liquid in the SA only increases.

In other cases, "victims" simply isolate themselves emotionally and do not react to attacks in any manner.

They may even seem devoid of feelings; however, *all of their feelings are just hidden inside.* They continue thinking about possible reactions to insults. This attitude clearly shows that these people *idealize something (relations, reasonability,etc.).* That is why, in addition to existing problems, the Guardians will apply educational measures to these people. These measures may manifest themselves as health problems or something even worse. The "victims" start to feel trapped because everything in their life goes wrong. It seems like they are on their way to an untimely departure from the Earth.

Is there a way out of this situation? As we imagine, people who are trying to isolate themselves should consider the "life is a circus" attitude and position themselves as spectators.

Yet, you have to understand that if *deep inside you remain overly emotional, there is no chance for you to leave the arena and stop performing with the other clowns.* That is why you should try to stay in the auditorium, watching your partners from a distance as they play the role of a control freak or house tyrant.

Without any doubt, he or she will try his or her best to pull you back into the arena and involve you in the performance.

He or she feels lonely without you and will look for new ways to bring you back.

Your main task is to not let anyone influence you. You may even imagine *that this person holds a lasso in his hands.* As soon as you lose vigilance, he will throw it over you and pull you back into the arena.

Consequently, while meeting with such people or even talking with them on the phone,

do not forget about the lasso, and do not allow yourself to get caught as a horse.

It is not very difficult. Just keep in your mind the picture of your opponent with the lasso.

It will help you to stay calm and make fun of the situation.

This method is very efficient. It will help you to remain a spectator, and as a result, your SA will not become filled.

Applying this Attitude

How can you apply the attitude we are suggesting? Use it every time you experience negative stress.

This attitude is especially good for housewives, scientists, and employees of large companies who are happy with their status and are not willing to change anything.

A businessman working at a project is better off assuming the "player" attitude, but only at work.

When he rests at home, meets with friends, plays with children, or works in a garden, he should apply the "life is a circus" attitude. Even at work, if he stresses out about a lack of money or the unreliability of his partners or employees, he behaves like a clown in the circus.

To relieve the stress, he might make a paper hat, write the name of his circus role on it, and place it on his desk. This hat will remind him not to return to the arena.

The same is true for a person unhappy with his position in a company or with his salary. While trying to achieve his goals, he should be a player, while the rest of the time he should be a spectator.

In many situations, we need to be emotional and goaloriented; however, it is very important to always keep a positive mood and never return to the circus arena wearing a funny hat.

If you do not have any goals in life, it would be even more ridiculous for you to become a clown. Just relax and watch the circus of life from a distance.

Summary

1. The first recommended attitude is called "life is a circus." To assume this attitude, you need to accept that everything happening in life is just a clown show in a circus arena. People fervently participate in the show, while you are a spectator watching them from a distance.
2. This attitude is different from going into denial because deep inside you do not suffer from stress or react to anything.
3. This attitude lets you change your perception of the situation, which seemed terrible before. If you look at this situation from a distance and make up a name for your funny role in the circus, then your situation becomes easily resolved.

3.2   Life Is a Game.

The next attitude we would like you to try in order to avoid idealizing earthly values is called "life is a game."

Everything Is a Game.

This attitude requires that *you consider events happening around you as different games.* For example, at home you may play a game called "family life" or "I am the man in this family." At the office, you play the game called "work" or "my own business." The games you play with friends are called "friendship" or "fishing;" with a girlfriend, it might be called "love," "sex," etc.

Why is this attitude good for you? It provides you with *an opportunity to not become excessively attached to any values.* Sometimes we win the game, but sometimes we lose. Try to consider all of your *good luck as a temporary victory and all of your bad luck as a temporary loss.*

For example, if you did not succeed in getting a desired position in a company, it just means that your competitor won the game this time. Yet, next time he will lose! Otherwise, you will defeat him in a different field as you try to get a higher position in a different company.

If your project does not work out well enough or you are in debt, think of it. Maybe *you are playing the wrong game.* You either have to change the terms of the game, admit your loss, or try to win a different game.

How to Cope with Misfortune

The attitude that "life is a game" may considerably decrease the amount of your stress, and as a result, you will not receive any "educational measures" from Life.

Professional players play an active role in games, but they do not suffer too much stress if they lose. They know that the next time, they will probably win.

This attitude is very effective, and many politicians and businessmen possess it. Look at successful government officials.

They know in advance that they will not be in power for a long time. Yet, they ardently play the managing game, sometimes gaining huge profits. Life does not care how you earn your living. You may earn a salary, profit from your business, or receive a gift from people you helped.

The emotions you feel and the idealizations that you possess are much more important.

If you are glad and thank Life for help, everything will be fine.

Yet, if you become arrogant or take offense, expect problems. Players cannot afford to be depressed for a long time because they will not have any time to play.

The "life is a game" attitude is also very popular among businessmen. They are serious about their work, but they still admit that losses are possible. Deep inside they are ready for a loss; that is why the successful businessmen take things easy and live their life to its fullest.

If you plan on becoming rich, choose a game that will let you earn your wealth as soon as possible. Just do not break the law while trying to reach your goals. For a while, you will have to forget about art, helping others, etc., because these things do not bring much money. You may pursue these things later, after you have earned as much as you want.

If your goal is doing creative work, however, then you need some other game that will let you create something new, despite the fact that it will probably not bring you much income.

Signs of a Game

You should not dedicate all of your time to playing games.

You should only play them *if you have a goal that you need to achieve.*

If you automatically do common things, it is not a game. Going to work, arguing with a husband (wife) or neighbor, and taking a vacation are not participating in a game.

Yet, these activities may become a game if you have some goal in mind. For example, if you want to make a career, you need to take certain actions toward achieving this goal; however, if you are passive and just wait for a promotion, it is not a game anymore. It is a circus performance in which you play the leading role.

Usual Games

In many countries of the world, there exists a set of rules concerning human behavior in a variety of situations—for example, business rules, rules of social or family behavior, and so on. If you want to participate in one of these games, *you have to observe the standard rules.* For instance, if you play a game called *"honest business,"* then you have to maintain the prestige of your firm, promptly pay all taxes, maintain the high quality of goods or services, etc.

On the other hand, if you decide to play a game called *"becoming rich at any cost,"* you probably will deceive your partner or the state, or steal someone's money by credit card fraud. In this case, what you would do next is try to avoid justice. Just keep in mind that all of this will lead to Life's punishment being cast upon you.

We all decide for ourselves what game we want to play based on our education, social status, personal goals, beliefs, and other factors.

A Personal Game

We may play *group games* (like "honest business"), but then we have to observe the rules; however, if you do not enjoy group games, you may start your own *personal game* with your own rules. It is possible that others will not understand you and even find you offensive. They believed you were playing according to the same rules. Yet, you have personal rules and have a right to change them at any moment.

Restrictions

When starting your own game, you should remember one restriction: *Do not break the main requirement of Life—do not judge others and yourself.*

For example, you are a single lady. You decided to participate in the "love" game and are trying to attract a man whom you like. If you attach excessive importance to the results of this game, your Guardian will not permit this man fall in love with you.

In accordance with the rules of this game, you must either admit defeat and start looking for a solution, or you need to participate in another game. Let us talk about the first option. Your decision should be based on the circumstances.

Maybe the man does not love you because he already has a girlfriend. Then you may wait and see; maybe they will break up, and you will be able to win him. You have to understand, however, that waiting may take a long time (even until the next life), and you should not let your SA overflow while you are waiting.

The attitude you assume while waiting is very important.

If you patiently wait for a convenient moment, everything will work out fine. You will be energetic and in a good mood. Your victory is guaranteed.

If you grieve over your unhappy love, however, you are already playing *a different game*
called "unhappy love."

Your life will become *even worse* to make you understand that unhappy love is not the worst thing in the world.

This "I am the unhappiest person" game has many different variations, yet all of them are based on the same idealization, which is self-imperfection. Life will apply strict measures to you for playing this game.

These results show why we should not play games that allow us to feel negative emotions and have negative thoughts. All of our games should result in a victory and positive emotions. Misfortune should be considered merely as a temporary defeat, and our positive emotions should remain with us.

Conventional Rules

Having the ability to change the rules of a personal game sounds very nice; however, there are *conventional rules* that we all should observe. For example, while playing a game, we should not commit any violence. (The Criminal Code says the same thing!)

Some people, however, do not care about the Criminal Code. You may try this approach if you wish. Yet, it means you entered the game called "who is more cunning?" and the police or tax officials may be pursuing you all the time.

Do not take offense if you lose this game because it was your own choice.

Inner Rules

In business, there are also *inner rules*. In large firms, these rules are called "corporate culture." If you work in a firm, you must observe these rules to be accepted. You may play your own games, but they should not break any company rules.

Otherwise, you will be let go. In small companies, however, bosses and employees seem to often play all kinds of dishonest games.

As a "player" in a game, *you may set any goals and strike to achieve them.* This attitude is perfect for decisive and confident people who are ready to take risks to achieve their goals. It works better for businesspeople than for officials or department chairmen, who have defined job responsibilities.

Any person, however, regardless of his occupation and temperament, can use this attitude to reach personal goals (marriage, work, purchasing a house, taking a vacation, etc.). Adopting this attitude will allow you to avoid accumulating additional stress while you are striving to achieve your goals.

Summary

1. The second attitude called "life is a game" allows us to avoid accumulating stress as we work toward accomplishing our goals.
2. This attitude presumes that, as we are working toward our goals, we are also prepared for possible defeat and will not take offense with Life if a loss occurs. Instead, we should try to win the next round of the game.
3. The advantage of this attitude is its effectiveness for people who are energetic and aggressive in reaching their goals, i.e., prone to breaking the main Life requirement.
4. People with other temperaments may also use this attitude to achieve their personal goals.

3.3   Life Is a Complex Mechanism.

Another attitude toward life is called *"life is a complex mechanism."* According to this attitude, we are all small parts of the big machinery of Life.

Applying This Attitude

In the workplace, people who work for large organizations that provide them with necessities and warranties, often have this attitude. Monasteries are also a good example, as well as many state organizations (including the army, police, and other government bodies where people may work throughout their life).

In private life, this attitude often means that, no matter what happens, you still believe that "everything God does is for the best" *and you totally accept the results.* If you get paid for your work, good; if not, that is the way it should be. If people love you, good, and thanks to God. If not, you probably do not deserve it. You humbly accept any turn of events without complaining or making negative statements.

No matter what happens, *you still enjoy life* and do not have any complaints. Your mind is free of stereotypes, and you accept Life as it is.

Requirements of This Attitude

Let us tell you right away that there are very few people with the above-mentioned attitude. Most people who have this attitude are very religious or monks (nuns).

Our education system makes us strong people fighting for our goals. We try to imitate people whom we see on television and who seemingly have power, enjoying a life filled with money, joy, sex, etc. Plenty of people enviously watch soap operas about the luxurious lives of millionaires. For these people, the only acceptable standard of living is being able to constantly fall in love, betray others, buy houses or beautiful cars, attend balls, and so on.

We are not claiming that this is bad. If you have enough money and can afford purchasing houses and attending balls non-stop, then go ahead! We came to Earth to try everything.

Yet, life is not only attending balls and having sex, even for the richest people in the world. They also have their own tasks, and if they do not fulfill them, "educational measures" will be applied to them. The Guardian does his job well.

We mean to say that all of those movies and television shows build a model of perfect living for us. So when our life does not fit that model, we start complaining and become unhappy. In other words, we *start idealizing that lifestyle.* You already know what happens to us in such situations.

Do not forget that the things we see on television are invented by people in Hollywood. These fairytales bring the filmmakers millions of dollars, while we just live in their imaginary world. It is not bad, but let us not get upset with reality. Instead, let us accept it as it is.

An extreme version of this attitude is the belief that we are all small components of a big mechanism called "Life."

This attitude makes us accept good and bad events with the same feelings. If you succeed in having this view, then no negative events will happen in your life because Life will have no reason to teach you lessons.

Requirements of Being a "Small Part"

You may have the attitude of being a "small part" if you work for a large and stable company. People working in such companies *must be extremely loyal and strictly adhere to the rules established in the company.* A company of this kind gives its employees a lot of security and confidence; that is why people who do not like risk are happy there, even if their salaries are not very high. They like the feeling of being *a part of a big mechanism* where they merely have to perform assigned duties and not break the work rules of the mechanism.

Large companies are very conservative. They *dislike innovations and initiative,* especially when they come from employees. If there are too many active employees in the company, they will hinder its smooth functioning. This is why large firms often fire employees who try to get promoted at any cost and think more about themselves than about the company's well-being. The company needs *total loyalty,* and if an employee is really loyal, then he will get raises, receive promotions, and one day even assume the *highest executive position—for example, CEO.*

If you start working for such company, be prepared to become a small part of a huge machine. If you realize it and do not feel any discomfort, and if you are sure that you will *never take offense* with the company for not appreciating you enough or for paying you too little, then this job is right for you.

Yet, if you have a higher opinion of yourself and want to try something creative, like being the Chairman of the Board of Directors, then this attitude is not good for you.

Pay attention to one of the two following attitudes: They will not allow you to excessively idealize earthly values, but you will be able to satisfy the desire of being a leader or a millionaire within a short time.

Applying This Attitude

You may assume the suggested attitude if you are not very confident and hope that *Life will give you everything you need anyway.* This attitude may be used in any domain of life—love, family life, work, hobbies, etc; however, such convictions are good for an employee, not for a Master of Life. They will not suit businessmen planning to fulfill a project.

This attitude is good for a smart official working in large state organization. He can have his own ideas, but should promote them in a way accepted in his organization, without taking offense if they do not understand or approve of his ideas. If he makes a considerable effort promoting it, sooner or later the situation will change for the better. It is just very important that, while making these efforts, he does not take offense with Life. We all know that attaching excessive importance to our ideas leads to our Guardian taking educational measures against us.

Differences and Similarities with Other Attitudes

On the surface, this attitude reminds us of the one called "life is a circus." Yet, there are certain differences between these attitudes. A person who is a "small part" cannot periodically go back to the arena and try to achieve his goals.

This person simply does not have goals in life that he wants to reach! He is satisfied with everything he receives and does not want anything else. So if you have unsatisfied desires and you fight for them, then you are not a "small part."

You are a player!

A spectator in the circus can always return to the arena and become a player again. Later, he may return to the audience. "Small parts" cannot do it. They belong to a big mechanism, and if they start functioning slower or faster, the mechanism will break. "Small parts" *do not have the right for independence;* they must work in coordination with other parts of the mechanism. If you are fine with this role, just remain a "small part." Maybe later you will be able to join others in the arena.

Summary

1. The third attitude is accepting life as a large mechanism of which we are all small parts.
2. This attitude is good for people who do not have any complaints about life and who accept all of its manifestations.
3. As a "small part," you may still set goals and aim at their achievement. Yet, you may only do it if you follow the rules that you have accepted in your life and do not break them.

3.4   Life Is What I Want.

The name of this chapter looks like the most attractive of all. Really, it is so nice to live when you can do whatever you want and choose whatever life you prefer. You may become an actor, an artist, a millionaire, or anything else.

The Choice Is Already Made.

Is it possible to choose a life that we could enjoy? The answer to this question is very simple. *You already live the life that was chosen by your soul a while ago.* If you are now unhappy about something in your life, your soul probably did not have many choices. Can you guess why?

The answer to this question is clear if we remember that the Subtle World consists of many levels in which the souls from the upper levels have more choices. They may choose everything they want.

Souls from the lower levels have much less choice. The more sins we bring with us when we die in one life, the less choices we will have in the next incarnation.

Accordingly, we have to solve many of our soul's problems and untangle several karmic knots. This sounds like a difficult life with only a little time for pleasures. It may become even worse if, during this incarnation, we accumulate more idealizations.

Some people know how to solve this problem. They just commit a suicide. Yet, it is just an illusion, not a real solution. Suicide sends our souls to the lowest level of the Subtle World, where they receive the proper treatment.

Then they are sent back to Earth to start a new, more difficult life. We already mentioned it before.

For these reasons, we had better *get rid of our sins while we are still on Earth.* We may try living the life we want only after we have solved all of our problems and untangled all of the knots.

As a result, *Life will only satisfy all of the desires of people whose SA is virtually empty*; however, even those people face some restrictions. They already live in this world and have to initiate changes *from their starting positions.*

Starting Positions

Hopefully, you understand what is meant by "starting positions."

It means our place of birth, race, where we live, our family, work, obligations, etc. Even with Life's best support, *it is impossible to considerably change the situation.*

If you live in a poor neighborhood, raise many children, and have no education, it is difficult for you to become a superstar, a successful doctor, or an outstanding banker.

Yet, it is not impossible. You may get divorced, and later meet and marry a banker's daughter. This is a good choice for a person who is not receiving any of Life's educational measures.

Yet, this idea does not sound very realistic. In real life, if a person does not have idealizations, it only means that *he or she is not very interested in earthly values.* That is why marrying a wealthy person and living a rich life hardly sounds attractive to him or her, as well as—let's say, robbing a bank.

That is why a person with little stress liquid in his or her SA will choose something very different, most likely working for others and not being paid much for it.

Does it mean that the attitude "life is what I want" is not available for people who have *a fuller SA?*

What to Do if You Are Not a "Saint"

No, it does not mean this at all. Of course, we all have to accept our starting conditions; however, it is possible to reach our goals more quickly without accumulating new sins.

We will mention some of the methods in the following chapter.

You need to understand *what exactly it is that you want to achieve. Create a plan for achieving your goals and move toward them with Life's help* and by making real efforts. Whatever goal you have, it is reachable, especially if you constantly smile.

Life does not care if you have two hundred dollars or two hundred million dollars. Compared to the total amount of money on our planet, these sums of money are too small. You will get as much money as is safe for your soul. Of course, you will only receive it if you observe the aforementioned rules and ask Life for help in a right way.

We will tell you more about this in the next chapter.

There are many ways to change our lives. We have only considered three types of attitudes that allow us to avoid attaching excessive importance to certain values and not collect additional stress. Yet, there may be more ways.

Each of us may choose his or her own attitude, taking into account his or her interests and needs. It is important to remember that this attitude should not let us idealize earthly values and should allow us to continue thinking positively.

We may live our lives the way we want. Let us just figure out what we really want and try to gain Life's help.

Summary

1. It is very easy for a person with an empty SA to live life the way he or she wants; however, these people are not demanding.
2. People with a fuller SA may improve their life if they follow the main requirements of Life and ask it for help correctly.
3. Each of us may develop his or her own attitude, taking into account his or her interests and needs, and not adding liquid to his or her SA.

4

How to Correctly Form the Events of Your Life

NOW WE ARE COMING TO THE LAST PART OF OUR book. Here we are going to tell you how you can use Life's good attitude toward you. Sometimes you feel that you are smiling at Life, and it smiles back at you. This is the best moment to give a hint to Life that you are lacking something for your complete happiness. You have to decide what it is yourself because Life itself has everything. It can give you money, talents, love, great relationships, a desired job, etc.

Theoretically, you can get anything that you want.

Practically, it's also absolutely possible—if you learn how to avoid the common mistakes. To request (order, form, or create) the desired events in your life requires a correct approach— otherwise the very request can result in unpredictable events. If you put a five-year-old kid behind the wheel of a Hummer and leave him alone, he will not be able to use the power and capability of this great vehicle, and his trying to drive can cause negative results.

The same thing happens to people who are trying to use the power and potential of Life itself, not being aware about the rules of communication with Life.

We offer you some recommendations that will help you to use all your potential to become Life's favorite child, getting the ultimate result for yourself.

What You Need in Order to Succeed

Many people are just interested in one thing—*how to carry out their desires as fast as possible and with minimum effort on their side.* Experience shows that it never happens that way.

Nevertheless, some people manage to keep their lives the way they want, and their problems seem to be solved on their own, while you are struggling with life. Maybe you need to be educated in a particular way?

Yet, life shows that, even in business, having graduated from a business school does not necessarily guarantee your success. Many people have MBAs, and it only helps them to find an okay-paying job at a big company.

The fact is that the majority of millionaires and billionaires do not have a special business education; they managed to make their first million dollars at some point without using any of the specialized knowledge taught in business schools.

Usually, possessing such character traits as determination, self-assurance, aggressiveness, and courage makes all the difference.

On the other hand, you might have seen many people who do possess some or all these character traits, but they do not have such a big success in life because they only use them during family scandals and defending their point of view while interacting with friends.

So, the character traits, as we see here, are also not the ultimate factor. Then what is it?

Why is it that only 5-8% of all new enterprises are successful?

To answer this question, let's relate to a notion called "*to be lucky*" or "to have a lucky hand." If you are that type, then anything you plan will come to fruition. If you are not, you will be struggling all the way through, getting more and more frustrated.

It was a superstition in the old times, and it remains to this day. You might have an excellent knowledge of marketing, financing, management, international law, and accounting, and your business still will not work out the way it should.

And vice versa—there are people that have it all at the snap of their fingers. They might not have a special education, but they have *luck*. You don't have luck, but boy, do you want to befriend it!

It concerns all aspects of life—doing business, finding your ideal partner in life, buying a house, going on vacation, etc.

We already talked about the reasons why luck avoids us (in the previous chapters of this book). So in this chapter you will find an answer to how to get Life's help (luck) to achieve your goals.

4.1   Three Conditions of Success

What do we have to do in order to fulfill our dreams? You can use the technique called the Method of Forming Events by Thought Power. It teaches you how to use Life's help consciously to make your dreams come true.

It's not very difficult; you just have to obey the rules of Life.

Therefore, to clear your problems and get what you want, you have to obey three important conditions:

- *Do not negate the outside world.*
- *Choose and accept a rightful position in Life.*
- *Arrange for correct interaction with Life itself.*

You can see that the first two conditions were thoroughly examined in the previous chapters of this book. The third condition is the subject of this chapter.

Great, you would say, but the question remains: In what aspects of life is it necessary to apply all three conditions? For instance, in business, maybe it would be enough just to ask Life for money, without going into the process of recognizing and eliminating our idealizations?

Which of those conditions should you pay attention to when looking for love or a higher- paying job? The answer is simple: *You have to obey all three of them at all times.*

Neglecting even one of them may lead to "educational measures" applied toward you, bringing more problems into your life, while complying with all three conditions is necessary for your life to become what you want it to be.

As we see, the mechanism of spiritual punishment is flawless and equally disciplines all of us, regardless of our good traits of character and even good deeds. You get what you deserve— no exceptions. If you have an idealization of money in this life and a big desire to have lots of money, the spiritual punishment will be applied to you, and you will lose your last money. By this punishment the hint is given to you that the well-being of your soul should be your priority, and then, and only after then, you will receive the fulfillment of your money dreams.

You can understand why it happens this way. From the point of view of our Guardian, our present life here is just a tour to planet Earth. He is only interested in arranging for your soul's well-being. So if he feels that he should cut short your "tour"—that is, your life—in order to save you, he will do it without hesitation.

Just imagine ending your life for some unknown and very far-fetched reasons. The Guardian will consider himself right in thinking that he took away your erroneous life (from his point of view). How about you?

Thus we recommend that you comply with all three conditions stated above, even if you have everything you need and do not desire anything more.

Summary

1. To achieve your goals quickly and effectively, you have to fulfill three conditions:
   - Do not negate the outside world.
   - Choose and accept a rightful position in Life.
   - Organize correct communication with Life itself.

2. Only fulfilling all three conditions is necessary and enough for reaching your goals.

4.2 Main Principles of the Method of Forming Events by Thought Power

The technique of reaching your goals at the level of unstoppable luck is called *Method of Forming Events by Thought Power.*

This Method was conceived and executed as an applied technological tool for complimentary interaction of a human being with Life when attaining his personal goals.

The term "complimentary interaction" means a harmonious way of moving toward your desired goals, rather than beating your head against the wall.

It is simple to understand why you should not be in contradiction with the outside world. We already know that the world surrounding us presents a fine-tuned and complex mechanism; it does not tolerate any crude acts and breaking of Life's rules. Crashing everything on the way to your goal would mean your complete ignorance and unwillingness to read the suggestions of your Guardian. Most probably, *you idealize (that is, exaggerate) your talents and abilities* regarding your planned goals, and as we know, it results in "educational measures" being sent your way.

To make the dreams come true effectively, we suggest paying attention to a few principles. If you are already familiar with the system of D. Carnegie (or systems similar to his), we suggest that you combine those systems with our principles, which, we are sure, will create a wonderful effect.

Various Sources

We would like to draw your attention to another important fact: Two different sources of Subtle World are responsible for watching us comply with Life's rules and helping us to reach our goals. We will talk about them later. At the base of our Method of reaching our goals using Life's help, we find *seven main principles of arrangement of the thoughts and actions of a human being.* Let's take a look at them.

4.2.1   First Principle: You Yourself Create All Events in Your Life.

This statement is easy to grasp, but it seems very dubious. How about our illnesses, troubles with family members, layoffs at work, inflation, high gasoline prices, etc.—all those things that spoil our everyday life?

Retrieve Your Experience

On the one hand, everything mentioned above seems to have nothing to do with us. On the other hand, we all participate in the whole process that created the abovementioned events. Each of you can recall a moment in your life when *you really wanted something, and then it happened*, though before the actual implementation of your wish there had not been any objective reasoning for the situation to unfold so happily for you.

For instance, somebody sent you a gift—something that you wished for secretly for a long time. Or you *suddenly* found a great job that you could only ever dream of having. Or you managed to go on vacation that you never thought you would find time or money for. Or you met a person who became the love of your life, overcoming against-all-odds circumstances.

Whether you believe it or not, you yourself attracted those good events into your life. Unfortunately, very often *we attract lots of negative events as well.* For example, you were afraid that you would not be able to pay a credit card, though you have a job and money is coming in; yet, suddenly you face problems with paying this credit card for no obvious reason. Or you were afraid to catch a cold during the flu season, so you took loads of vitamin C and dressed sensibly for the weather; yet, you caught a cold or the flu, no matter how much you tried to stay healthy.

Have you ever caught yourself, while planning an event, actually imagining dozens of negative outcomes, at the same time trying to find dozens of possible defenses for those negative results? What happens in reality is that some other negative deviation of your event that you had not even imagined takes place, and you fail.

If you take into serious consideration everything that we said earlier in this book, you can understand that the *negative result that occurs as a consequence of your indirect fears, or as an outcome of the "educational measures," is sent to you by your Guardian to help you to destroy an idealization* (in this case, an idealization of control of the outside world). You take your plans too much to your heart; you are sure you are able to control any part of your planning under any circumstances. So your Guardian has to destroy this idealization.

Being sincere with yourself will help you to realize a simple idea that *everything happening to you in this life is an outcome of your mental acceptance or planning.*

Here is another example. A young lady complains that the money she is making is not enough. When asked how much she would like to earn, she answers with a particular dollar amount, but also adds at the same time that she *does not* believe that somebody will pay her that much. If she herself does not believe that she can make that amount, who else will believe it? If nobody believes it, nobody will offer her the desired salary.

The negative programming circles, and she has the life she has, with the salary she is unhappy about. There is only one way out— she can help herself to break that vicious circle.

There are a thousand examples like this, when people consider themselves offended, insulted, sick, unworthy, having no talents, etc. No wonder that in their real lives they get what they are stuck with in their minds and never can have their wishes fulfilled.

Rule One

The conclusion is this: **Think positively!** This rule should become a building block of your mental process.

Thinking positively means *seeing* yourself in your thoughts the way you want to be— healthy, beautiful, wealthy, and happy.

If you have an important meeting and you are afraid to get a negative answer from the people you depend on, visualize mentally several *positive* variations of this meeting. It does not matter if you still cannot imagine this meeting as being friendly or pleasant, but it is imperative to imagine a positive ending of the meeting. Create Hollywood in your head; predicting a *happy end* for your story and its probability will manifest itself in a positive outcome in your real life.

If your mind is loaded with fears and apprehensions, you can be sure that everything that you are so afraid of will most likely happen (especially if these fears concern you personally).

As we said before, even if you imagined all possible ways of dealing with a possible negative result, Life will invent yet another harmful tactic to turn the events the way you could not possibly predict.

You cannot keep away from it because it was you who drew in this negative event by your own unreasonable thoughts and fears.

Hence, the solution is simple: **Always wait for and imagine positive results**, no matter how many variations of the event you can play in your mind. Life itself is selfcontained, it has everything anybody needs, and it has an abundance of everything.

Since your requests equal your thoughts, then thinking "I will not succeed, anyway," "This is not for me," or "I missed my chance," will result in Life giving you exactly what you asked for: You will not succeed, it will not be for you, and you will have no chance.

Instead, use your potential to create positive thoughts, which will become the construction blocks of your happy future.

Examples of Applying Rule One

For instance, you are unhappy about your salary, and you would like to earn more money. Usually, a person in this situation has harsh mental conversations with his boss or discusses his decisions and abilities with colleagues. This senseless and energy-draining process only points out his idealizations (idealization of money, abilities, or relationships).

To achieve this goal, all he has to do is to imagine that he comes up with some constructive proposal at work, that his boss compliments him, or that he is being promoted to a better position.

If it is impossible at his place of work, then he can envision that he receives a tempting offer from another company, and he changes his job. The more intense his thinking is, the more positive possible options he can create in his mind, and the sooner those "fantasies" will turn real.

You can apply this technique to any situation in life. If you are lonely, do not dwell on your self-pity (for it is an erroneous belief called Taking Offense with Life). Try to imagine a story in your mind of meeting the man/woman of your dreams or your future spouse. Make up all the little details about how it will happen, where, and how it will develop. Within a few months of such positive thinking, you will create the desired event, and your loved one will just appear.

One of our readers could not get pregnant for many years. The doctors could not help, and she and her husband had lost all hope. Then she changed her inner motivation and decided that she was *already* pregnant; the only difference was that it was taking a bit longer than it should have. She started walking like a pregnant woman, touching her belly, and talking to an imaginary baby inside. Four months later, she got pregnant and later had a healthy baby boy. Her positive self-programming turned out to be stronger than the knowledge of her doctors.

Let's not talk about the negative events in our life like fire, theft, getting into a really bad car or plane crash, or being a victim of terrorists. It's obvious that you never had them on your mind; they just were sent to you as "educational measures" by your Guardian.

Before we disclose the next principle of a human being's arrangement of his thoughts and actions, we would like to tell you which inhabitants of the Subtle World help us in reaching our goals. When our long-term dreams come true and we regard them as miracles, it is apparent that we cannot see the heavenly mechanics and those who actually generated our desired events and sent them our way. We cannot see them because they exist in an invisible domain parallel to our world.

4.2.2   Who Helps Us Generate Our Desired Events?

It is clear that nobody knows exactly how the Subtle World is organized and what particular creatures inhabit it. There are many religious and esoteric versions on this account, with no trace of proof from the point of view of modern science.

Yet, if science cannot prove or refute the existence of a believed phenomenon, it does not mean that it really does not exist. It only means that discovering the existence if this phenomenon stays at the stage of possibility in the domain of our real world.

It is interesting that all the interpretations of the Subtle World are equally effective. In religion, by entrusting his being to God (Saints, Gurus, Masters, Heavenly Fathers, Jesus Christ, Allah, etc.), every believer gets support and help according to his faith.

4.2.3   Second Principle: Climb only one peak!

The second principle of *the arrangement of the thoughts and actions of a human being* states: "Climb only one peak!" or "Run in only one direction."

Everybody is torn by many wishes and desires, which change even within one day. That is why our sponsoring egregors hardly have time to fulfill one of our dreams, when we are already on the run demanding other things.

This is what we do our whole life.

The Problem of Multiple Wishes

If you try to examine your thoughts and desires within a certain period of time, you will definitely find out that you want everything at the same time.

All these wishes come to us according to new information we receive all the time. These wishes are replaced by other ones that are to be replaced by yet other ones later. It means that your desires are not arranged in their priority, and it looks like you are trying to run in many directions at the same time.

Make an effort to sit down and recall the scope of desires you had today, yesterday, last week, and last month.

Do you have the ones that are consistent on your list?

What form and shape (positive/negative) have you used to express these wishes?

By doing this simple drill, you will realize how hard it is for your egregors to help you. Your patron cannot run in all those directions, making all your wishes come true at the same time— he just does not have enough power for that.

To be more precise, he could, but by spreading himself thin, he won't be able to effectively perform your wishes on a desired level. As to you— you do not even support him by your energy because your thoughts and wishes are not focused on a certain goal for more than five minutes.

Choose one wish (or several, but in the same direction), and load your egregor with the task of performing only these important wishes.

On the other hand, in order to not lead him astray and not to be in his way, hold back your other wishes for the time being.

Visualize only one hilltop, and imagine yourself climbing it. Most probably you won't even need to conquer another one afterwards.

4.2.4   Third Principle: Go with the Flow!

This principle suggests you choose from your wish list the very wish that is easiest to work out at the moment.

We Are Not Alone.

This principle came as a conclusion that we are not alone this world. If you have a desire to find a new good-paying job, and you even are trying to do it according to the techniques of this book (that is, make your egregor find you this job fast), it is not the fact that it will happen immediately.

Such a situation exists because, besides you, *there live billions of people in the world who, for their parts, are also looking for something at this very moment—they also wish for something, and they also act.* They do all of that without any system, in absolute chaos—they themselves run many directions. According to their multiple desires, their egregors are also in a rush to perform their duties. It all hinders your progress and stands in the way of your own egregor.

Streams of Subtle Energy

Nevertheless, we are not saying that in the Subtle World everything is done with no consideration to Earthly orders.

In reality, when big groups of people are involved in one idea or execute a well-thought plan, then they are able to create purposeful streams of energy with the help of many various egregors, which influence the rise and fall of empires and countries, the economical change on the market, the construction of colossal enterprises, etc.

That is, in the Subtle World there exist *powerful streams of energy* that you'd better stay away from when trying to make your own wishes come true.

The better policy is to adjust to these invisible streams and use their commanding capacity to your maximum advantage. This is the main essence of our third principle: *Go with the flow.*

The idea is quite simple and should not raise any objections.

So how do we put it into practice? We cannot see physically the Subtle World's energy streams, can we? So we are not aware where they are flowing today and how they will change their direction tomorrow. Then what should we do?

How to Enter the Stream of Energy

We have a plain answer to this tricky question: listen to the signals of Life, and do what feels effortless to do today.

You all have lots of things to do on your agenda, don't you? You constantly need to choose what you need to take care of today or tomorrow, or later in the year. So we recommend you do the easiest thing today if, of course, this does not come in conflict with your official obligations, duties, or other objective circumstances.

For example, you have to meet a person and get some answer from him, but it seems that you are failing to reach him—he is on a business trip, is at a meeting, is sick, etc.

It means you are getting some information that your interaction with him would be undesirable or unproductive, and it won't give you the needed results. Of course, you can be persistent, come to his door, and stay there in your.

You finally see him, the results will be negative. Within our system, we recommend that in such dead-end situations you wait for the new development of the same event or try to find a way around to reach the results you expect, acting through intermediates or contacting this person via different organizations, etc.

What Happens When You Go against the Flow?

If you still decide that you will break your head against to wall and reach this person, eventually, this will not end well. The reason is that, *by building all those abovementioned obstacles on your way, Life points you to the issues that you did not foresee or did not think about.* It gives you a direct answer that the result you are expecting will not be achieved at this time.

You definitely have the right to establish your goals and make an effort to work them out, even if you meet all sorts of obstacles on the way. It is called being persistent.

Yet, in this case, such behavior will indicate that you do not want to decode Life's signs, relying solely upon your own being. Again, you have the right to do it, but then you have to realize that you are indeed *alone*, and Life will not help you by sending you luck. So we would not recommend this stubborn way of doing things because the outcome of your actions will be unpredictable.

If you still are determined to act this way, at least obtain a "salmon attribute"—this fish does go against the water stream, but it is using all the idiosyncrasies of the stream, using it to its advantage to get where it needs to be.

Recognize the Subtle Signs

You can easily define if you are moving against the flow *if you pay attention to the events and circumstances connected to the issue in question or your wish.*

Let's say you are trying to get someone on the phone but you get a busy signal all the time, or you got the person on the phone but he is not expecting your call—this *is* a sign that Life wants you to take into consideration.

The given example presents regular events happening in our everyday life. There is no way we recommend you to stop calling after the first busy signal. We realize that achieving goals in life does involve overcoming difficulties and utilizing inner energy. We simply urge you to consider and analyze the information about your vital issues according to what possibilities you can create using the *Third Principle*. Do not try to break through closed doors— look for an open one nearby.

The information from Life is flowing toward us constantly, but most of us are not used to decoding it and making decisions considering this information.

It happens quite often that you are determined to buy something. You get into your car and drive to the store, and all the stoplights on your way are red, you get into a traffic jam, or other circumstances hold you back. Maybe Life is trying to supply you with the information that you do not need to go to that store because whatever you want to buy there is not in stock or is defective—and probably you will have problems with this item later. *Similar signs are all around us.* All we need to do is develop an ability to see them.

What Kind of Signs Should We Take into Consideration?

You might have a question now: To what kinds of signs should I pay attention? If I leave the house and it starts raining, is it considered a sign that I need to go back?

Nobody wants to get paranoid trying to comprehend every single bit of incoming information.

Certainly, you only have to pay attention to the *strong and obvious signals* that provoke your inner resistance and irritation. If stopping on red at every stoplight on the way makes you aggravated, you definitely can interpret this as a sign.

The criterion for the authenticity of the signs of Life lies in your bodily sensations in the form of irritation or dissatisfaction.

You can ignore all other "signs" if they don't invoke such sensations inside you. If you ignore the *strong and obvious signs*, be aware that, in addition to your determination to make your dreams come true, you generate unnecessary negative emotions, and you yourself are responsible for them.

If you do use the *Third Principle* to form the events of your life while *minimizing all resistance and conflicts*, then it will be easier for your egregors to help you to attain the most wanted results in the ambiance of continual luck.

4.2.5 Fourth Principle: Befriend Your Egregor.

This principle recommends you never to forget about your higher patrons, regardless whether you ask them for help or not.

Help Your Egregor.

As we already told you, each of us, deliberately or not, is entangled in the relationship with multiple egregors, which we have formed in the course of our life through our certain upbringing, education, professions, hobbies, family ties, etc.

Each of these egregors helps us to attain success within our abilities and interests. It does not mean that we ourselves should not help our egregor to build his might and strength because he feeds on our thoughts and emotions. So if you deliberately cleanse the channel that connects the two of you, and send your love and gratitude toward your egregor, he grows more powerful and takes care of you more rigorously.

We urge you *to be a friend to your egregor!* Think about him more often, ask for a piece of advice, try to translate the information he sends you, and look for the results of his participation in your life. Do not be shy about asking him any questions—being in the Subtle World, he already knows your past, present, and future in all possible variants. His answers may come in a shape of very delicate thoughts, a line in a book or newspaper that you run across out of the blue, images on your television screen, or a fraction of overheard conversation between some strangers on the street.

How Egregors Help Us

Your egregor does not exist as a material matter; he cannot send you a written report on his activity about your life issues.

If we were extrasensory, could get rid of our little internal dialogue in our head on demand, and knew how to calm down our psyche, then the egregors could simply upload the sought-after-information inside our mind, like attaching a file when sending an email.

Yet, people are not extrasensory. Their bodies are littered by consummation of meat and alcohol, they smoke and take medicine, they do drugs and sink into countless passions, and they do not hear their inner selves.

So the egregors resort to using more complicated arrangements in order to deliver their valuable information.

Having gotten your request, the egregor can scan the immediate future events of your life, choose among them an element of a particular event that could suit you the most at this time, *and convey this element to you* in the form of a thought, a line in a book, etc.

If you are receptive enough to accept this information, you can establish a steady and fruitful communication with your egregor.

Address All Your Problems to Your Egregor

Consistent communication with your egregor will bring order to your personal life. For this, *you have to learn to assign the solution of your problems to your egregor and wait* while *he executes it.* It is most important to remain relaxed and to believe that your problems will be solved.

Religious believers all over the world use this very mechanism when they address their concerns to the Higher Power or God. God is known to be almighty, and if you ask him for something, then he will make your wishes comes true. If he does not succeed, then nobody will. This idea can help you to loosen up and part with your fears (this way, you stop envisaging a negative outcome), while waiting for the completion of your request. If you think positively, then eventually (with the help of the egregors) you will form the desired event.

According to the Second Principle, it is not advisable to burden your egregor with too many problems and wishes; otherwise, he will have to spread himself thin, which will produce a weak effect.

It is better to build your life using the *Third Principle, and try not to come up with a brand new wish every five minutes. You should load the egregor* only with the most serious issues that he will be to solve on time and to the best degree.

Don't be discouraged when the very development of the desired event does not look like you had imagined: Your egregor knows better than you how to carry out the plan.

Also, when you face a situation in which some of your requirements have not been observed, remember that the reason might be that Life itself is telling you that those requirements could be erroneous or inconsistent.

Lucky Days

We all have our lucky days when it seems that our problems are solved on their own. Such days show us how close we can get to our egregors at that moment. On those days you are riding the wave of a strong energy stream of your egregor, who removes other harmful energy streams and works in your favor.

Unfortunately, these lucky days are rare, but if you learn to communicate with your egregor and strengthen your energy field, then the number of these days will radically increase, and you will be able to put off some of your problems' solutions till your lucky days.

Do Not Reject Options.

Try not to lose possible chances! If you come across an option to change your job or meet a new person, if you are offered to go on an unexpected trip, or if you are given a new book or a thing, *do not rush to brush it off.*We are too much used to launching our logical thinking when getting a new piece of information, trying to define immediately what to do with it, i.e. we are used to make decisions only using the left side of the brain that rules our rational thinking.

How often has it happened that you rushed into making a logical decision and refused an offer, proposal, or even your own idea, only to scratch your head in disappointment later, reproaching yourself for that unwise decision?

So this simple tenet warns you about not making decisions solely based on raison d'etre.

Who knows, it is probably your egregor contacting you by that unreasonable idea (perhaps your wish that you had asked for long time ago). Perhaps he has worked out your longforgotten wish, and now is giving you a chance to finally make it happen; however, you foolishly turn around and ignore his efforts.

The recommendation here would be *to attempt to recognize this new information at least to some extent and see what will come out of it.* If the outcome will manifest itself in disorder, mistakes, and discrepancies, you can be sure it is not your way; probably it was somebody else's egregor trying to use you as a cog in his machine.

On the other hand, it can indeed be your egregor's information, but due to some unpredictable circumstances, the events took the wrong turn, so he is calling off the whole plan.

Taking into consideration all of the above, be sure you make at least a slight effort to decode information about new options that you have received before declining them, so you will not feel sorry later about missing your chance.

Advantages of Being Friends with Your Egregor

A person who is in contact with his egregor and trusts him fully is serene and peaceful; he stops being unreasonably nervous about political events, inflation, inadequate salary, and so on. He doesn't possess a deceitful idea that he totally controls his life and that everything only depends on him.

Such people are usually rewarded galore: They get a high-paying job, somebody returns them a forgotten debt, they follow a scoundrel-free path, they never buy a ticket for the plane bound to crash, etc.

4.2.6   Fifth Principle: Be strong.

The Fifth Principle of *the arrangement of the thoughts and actions of a human being* suggests that you be strong mentally (it would be great to be strong physically, too) on your path to succeeding in life.

"Being mentally strong" implies accepting the very subtle energy that we sense in the air, coming from other people, nature, egregors of different kinds, the cosmos, or other sources. In various systems, it is called "bio energy," "Prana," "Chi," etc.

Our modern technological society, pampering man's powerlessness, prevents us from finding effective ways to further develop this energy that can take care of our sensory field and health. Energy abilities of a modern man are limited.

Meanwhile, this is our energy level that identifies our utmost thoughts and emotions, locates our egregors, and defines the speed of the completion of our needs and desires.

Who Executes Our Orders?

If you are in contact with the low-level egregors of violence, drugs, etc., they will be your servants. They will put you on a vicious circle, and you are to come back to the same wish after you previous wish has been granted to you.

Average people without vice usually deal with *mid-level egregors* who provide them with average living conditions (house, couple of cars, middle-price furniture, college degree, miscellaneous common hobbies, family wellbeing, etc.). These people live in unconscious interaction with their egregors and do not feel any extra feelings toward their neighbors, and they do not strive to create anything new in their life. They are satisfied with their way of living, stable job, and guaranteed salary. This category of people presents the majority of the population in well-developed countries.

Other people are not satisfied just with this average "vegetation" kind of being, and they try to create something new in many aspects of life. Or, they feel a higher love toward people, animals, or nature—*these kinds of people are placed under a special protection of high-level egregors of creativity, science, mercy, and love.*

Finally there are other people serving religions (except for small sects that drag people into their organizations and make them walking zombies, "programming" their own followers), who have an ability to interact with the highest and most powerful egregors. They can work miracles and are called Prophets. As you understand, these people have an almost empty Stress Accumulator.

People who are in touch with the highest egregors present a group of strong Event Generators.

On the one hand, when they get in contact with their patrons, they do not care about the issues that worry an average person—money, living conditions, power, politics, relationships, etc.

On the other hand, they have a real opportunity to get "anything a soul could desire," but their soul does not desire what regular people usually dream about.

The Importance of Energy Burst

We would like to cheer up the readers who have already realized that they are quite far from being in a state of Prophets. In order to become a powerful Event Generator, you don't necessarily need to contain a prominent energy field at all times. *It is enough to generate it during those moments when you set up your goals and send your order to your egregor.*

Ordinary people at times accumulate a scope of Prophet energy, too. Luckily or sadly, they only feel it *during very strong emotional outbursts* that, as a rule, are caused by fear, when people face a real threat to life.

Unfortunately, when a person climbs a tree when trying to run from a dog that could bite him, he is not able to realize that at this exact moment he holds a very high level of vital energy that he can direct toward the Higher Powers—energy enough to actualize his wishes about hitting the lottery or finding that great job he dreamed of.

Similar energy eruptions take place at the moments of feeling overwhelming joy, love, or wrath. Yet, also during those moments, people *do not remember about their immediate problems and desires, and they plunge fully into the torrent of intense emotions.* The contradiction here lies in the fact that, if a person constantly keeps in mind his ardent desires, he is not able to experience any fervent emotions, and thus cannot find an opportunity to form the desired event. At the same time, this contradiction gives a clue for solving the problem of the accumulation of the energy field.

Sexual contacts for creating the events of your life. One of the partners (usually the less emotional one) could keep in mind the "order" during the intimacy with his/her partner.

Keep in mind though, that due to the narrow "qualification" of that egregor, he can only use his specific potential to make your wishes come true. So you can imagine what would happen if you did not devise correctly your "order."

Accumulate Your Energy

As we already told you, a regular person in our world does not usually have much energy at his disposal, being loaded with his domestic problems, getting sick, not exercising much, etc. The mental signal he is trying to send to his egregor is weak, and it is lost among millions of similar signals. If you want to be heard, *you have to shout louder than everybody!*

You can do it, if you manage to stop your inner sensations, worries, and idle thinking that actually take a lot of vital energy from you. You have to charge yourself consciously and then use the energy while channeling your wishes to the egregor. If your signal is loud enough, then the egregor will drop everything and will rush to complete your very order. Easy to say, hard to do, but do it and remember the *Fifth Principle: Be strong.*

Accumulate your energy and spend it wisely according to your set goals. It means, if you defined your goal and planned the ways of reaching it, you have to address Life using maximum energy. You can do it if you learn to increase the energy power of your body by doing special exercises and drills. Or you can save your energy for some time and then use it all at one point to address your egregor. The more powerful you are, the faster your dreams and wishes will be actualized.

4.2.7 Sixth Principle: Do Not Bustle.

Sometimes you feel that this bad luck is following you everywhere, but take a look at this issue from a different point of view.

Perhaps the circumstances you find yourself in today were created for you *so that you would learn to find a way out of the situations like these.* This skill will help you further in life to attain your success. It is also a possibility that your desires are much bigger than your real potential, and you will not be able to actualize them in the foreseeable future.

For instance, you want to become the president of your company, but at the same time, you are very shy and have no administrative skills. Wishes like this are usually not workable without special training.

Just try to believe your destiny and accept with gratitude everything that happens to you, and under no circumstances hold grudges in case of an undesirable turn of events. This way you will be sticking to the Main Rule, and good fortune will eventually come to you.

Failure Is Your Savior.

Very often our life saves us from bigger misfortunes, arranging several small troubles for you according to the fill of your SA. Being selfish, we can only interpret these troubles as the biggest misery on Earth.

For example, you suddenly got sick and could not attend an important meeting or a date. You regard this event as a huge nuisance in your life.

In reality, what happened was that Life was trying to protect you from a bigger negative stress and failure in the future. It is possible that you had predicted a very pleasant outcome of this meeting/date, while actually Life saved you from a bankruptcy or sexual harassment lawsuit.

At the moment of your distress, you cannot evaluate the situation objectively because it seems to you that you do not control the situation. In fact, what happened is good kismet that you cannot appreciate.

Interrelations of events in our life are so complex that very often we are not able to see the real picture, but we can learn to trust the natural course of events and search with appreciation for a sign of fortune in each incident occurring to us. Live by the saying: "Whatever God brings is to the better."

Watch Your Attitude.

Another aspect of the Sixth Principle advises you to watch your inauthentic attitude toward people around you.

When being a manager, before firing a seemingly unprofessional employee, point his mistakes out to him, and prepare him for the idea that he will need to change his place of employment. Do not break up the relationship abruptly; to do so would create a negative wave that could wash you off the shore on the way back.

Everything Is Interconnected.

When you act in a harsh way toward somebody, having your immense self-confidence, you consider this person only a physical entity that, according to your opinion, is behaving incorrectly—thus, you resort to the arsenal of your "educational measures" toward this person.

In reality, as we already told you, *every one of us,* even the most unworthy (to our opinion), *is linked by a set of energy strings to the Higher Powers*—his egregors of family, work, hobbies, alcoholism, religion, sex, etc. All his actions are a result of some integrated or segregated functioning of his egregors. Each of these egregors has his own plan how to operate this person in the future.

When you have animosity against this person, you interfere with this link, making some strings taut or breaking others. It definitely irritates the egregors linked to this person because you destroyed their plans concerning him.

Most of them, having lost the connection with their protege, will switch to you in discontent, looking for ways.

Try to recall a case of breaking up with somebody.

How soon afterward did *you find yourself stuck with some kind of problem* that you never even thought had anything to do with this break up? Now you have a tool to examine the past and re-evaluate this particular event from the point of view of our system. We are quite sure you will find the connection.

We urge you not to forget the Sixth Principle when you build your relationships with other people, no matter what the nature of these relationships may be—within your family, at work, or purely incidental.

It is true in correlation to your own self as well. Do not harbor hard feelings toward yourself; otherwise, you will destroy the plans of your own egregors about you.

4.2.8 Seventh Principle: God has no other hands but yours

Your thoughts are very valuable, especially when you deliberately organize your mental processes on the issue of forming events in your life. Yet, thinking alone without taking steps in the direction pointed to you by the Higher Powers will complicate the work of your egregors.

People Are the Hands of Egregors.

Egregors consist of the subtle substance that is formed by the product of our thoughts and emotions. This substance is very blank and frail and is not able to even hold a speck of dust in the air. Egregors' hands are people living in the real world, and his instruments are the thoughts in people's minds.

To form a certain event, an egregor should first plan each step, then *find the perpetrators and inspire them to some actions needed for the victorious implementation of the plan.*

As you can guess, it is not so easy to do. People are obstinate and are always guided by their own rules and ideas.

This way the actualization of *your* specific event can drag for a long time, especially if you do not help your egregor by doing real things in the real world.

The Seventh Principle encourages you to help your egregor help you.

Examples of Real Steps in the Real World

Let's say you are looking for a husband or wife. According to our Method, you have already made up the whole image in your mind and are waiting for the order to be done. If you really wish for this to happen, it can come about very quickly, especially when you actively assist your egregor to make it happen. He can find an appropriate partner and try to organize your meeting, but you yourself must look for this occurrence, widening the range of possibilities by meeting new people; going to resorts; attending parties, concerts, and shows; and going to other places where your egregor can get dynamic and inventive.

If you stay at home or shy away from men/women, then where is the chance for your egregor to find you a partner?

The same pattern works regarding all orders. Having asked your egregor for money, it is hardly so clever to sit at home waiting for a delivery of a likely a long-term prospect.

Otherwise, you would have to create such a strong energy outburst "to shatter the skies" that all available egregors would drop everything to complete your order. Do you have this power? Probably not.

That is why, after sending your "order" for money, you have to take active steps toward earning a big sum of money or at least toward creating conditions in which your egregor will be able to help you. For instance, you can start buying lottery tickets every day or begin looking for a higher-paying job. Then all your egregor has to do is to assure that the amount of money you receive would match your original request.

Please do not imagine that the egregor of gambling is willing to give you a multi-million- dollar jackpot only because you asked for it. These big winnings are usually destined for those people who dedicate themselves to gambling for a long time, and they get rewarded for their ardent loyalty to their egregor.

Nevertheless, even if you feel that you are far from being adept at gambling, you still have a chance to win.

Your immediate energy desire to hit the jackpot should equal the level of desire of one who has dedicated himself to this dream for many years.

As to the small winnings that some people get, they refer to a slightly different heavenly mechanics, which we will reveal later in this book.

These are the basic principles of the mental process of a human being and his conflict- free interaction with the real and Subtle World.

Summary

1. The best way of achieving your desired goals is a conflict-free communication with the outside world with the help of Life itself.

2. *We are helped by egregors—the inhabitants of the Subtle World; they are created by a group of people who are on the same wavelength.*

3. When trying to achieve his goals, a person should construct his thoughts and deeds in such a way that they would not overload his egregors, and that could allow them to focus on solving his most important problem.

4. To achieve the maximum effect in communication with one's egregor, one should be guided by the following basic principles.

4.3. Stages of Learning the Method of Forming Events

We already told you about the main principles that you should use to get the support of Life. The question remains: Is it enough just to be aware of them and try to use them in your life? The answer is that you have to develop some special abilities within yourself first, making an effort to learn these skills. Just for you, we have prepared an ultimate step-by-step system to learn the Method of Forming Events by Thought Power. It includes the following:

- Learning to relax your physical body
- Stopping your train of thought on demand.
- Detecting and recognizing real life goals.
- Enhancing your inner energy and self-assurance.
- Achieving your needed results.

Using this knowledge will eventually develop an automatic response in your being, and it won't take a huge effort to operate this Method. At first you will need to watch the offered sequence of the techniques, so they will become a part of you mind. Then you can start using them whenever you feel you have to "climb another peak."

Man is an inconsistent being. Every time his wish comes true, he feels it is not enough, and he longs for more. We always want something, every second of our life, and our egregors are at our service, provided we play by the rules.

Problems with Interaction with Egregors

As we already mentioned, each of us is in a constant interaction with other people, as well as with various egregors who are trying to influence our behavior, views, or decisions.

The stronger this interaction, the more opportunities we get to achieve anything we want in our life. The interaction with high-level egregors manifests itself in outbursts of intuition, revelations, inspiration, and at times, straight answers in a form of visions or perceived sounds. The problem with recognizing this communication lies *in the specific functioning of our brain to constantly produce thoughts.*

Our Restless Mind

Try to be present for a couple of minutes to what is going on in your head. Problems, memories, conversations, arguments, and fantasies are attacking you all at the same time! Our mind is restless; it renders an incessant internal dialogue that we can hardly control. This internal dialogue blocks our perception to identify the suggestions and hints sent by our egregors.

You probably can recall a situation in your life when you had to make a decision, and it somehow shaped in your head as a weak but promising idea, but then it was immediately washed away by a wave of logical thinking, calculations, and doubts, resulting in making the wrong decision. Later you wondered why you did not nourish that original idea and felt sorry. We can tell you: That idea was a piece of information sent to you by your egregor; he tried to give you a hint, but you rejected it because *your mind could not properly detect this weak energy signal.*

Besides, the sensitivity of our physical body is drastically decreased by stimulants like coffee, alcohol, nicotine, medicine, drugs, etc. So for increasing your body's ability to recognize the energy signals, we recommend a drill that will help you to stop the internal dialogue in your head, even if for a few minutes.

Relax Your Body.

Your mind is connected to your body. If you have a physical pain or tension, your mind constantly drags your attention to that area.

Learning to relax your body is imperative for learning to calm down your mind in order to halt your internal dialogue. It does not matter how you do it: with the help of a relaxation CD or breathing exercises—the key is you have to learn how to relax your muscles in two to three minutes, so no discomfort or aching in your body can distract you from the mental exercise. We urge you to do it, especially in the beginning of your training.

Calm Down Your Mind

After you learn how to relax your body, the next step is to hold your train of thought. It is not as easy as you might think, though there are many effective methods developed through centuries. They can be grouped as the following:

- *Technique of replacing thoughts* (by other repetitious thoughts)
- *Technique of focusing your mind on one object*
- Technique of conscious suppression of thoughts

Technique of Replacing Thoughts

The essence of this technique is in *replacing your chaotic thoughts with a certain phrase or sound combination.* In the Eastern school, they practice repeating so-called mantras, like "Omm," "Omm mane padve huum," or others.

Repeating your chosen mantra for a long time will place you in a different state of mind where you will be capable to detect your hidden psychic abilities and establish a working contact with your egregor. All religious prayers (particular words in particular combination) work the same way if you pray sincerely and rigorously for a long time.

You can use this technique to stop your relentless thoughts by continuously repeating a mantra or your own word combination.

Technique of Focusing Your Mind

The next method, well known in esoteric and religious science, *involves concentration of your mind on one object or process that you choose.* It can be a dot on the wall, a picture or a drawing, or your breathing or heartbeat. In Zen Buddhism, they practice the counting of one's own breathing. You can mentally count on inhale (harder) or exhale (easier) from one to ten, and then start all over. As simple as it seems, it takes an effort not to lose count and to do it for at least twenty minutes.

This exercise helps to develop your attention, which is a necessary condition for shutting down your internal dialogue.

The main requirement when doing this exercise is the *absence of any thoughts about your concentration.* You simply have to be present to your inner sensations without molding them into words. For example, you can focus your attention on the tip of your nose, trying to feel your breathing—how deep the air gets inside, if your nose feels warm or cold, etc.

Try to peacefully observe this process, rather than generate thoughts like: "Here, I am breathing through my nose, it is cold, and I feel the air coming inside my nose..."

If some thoughts start piling in your head, you will need to chase them away or simply wait for them to leave on their own. If you do this drill for twenty minutes a day, you will soon reach a steady result and will be capable of locking your internal dialogue for five to ten minutes at a time.

Technique of Conscious Suppression of Thoughts

This drill entails generating particular images in your mind in order to stop your internal dialogue.

For instance, you can imagine taking a towel and "wiping" all your thoughts in your head. The minute a new thought enters, you clean it the same way. Or you can "use" a vacuum cleaner or a net to catch the "intruder."

Your images can be of any kind, provided they are not accompanied by any tangible phrases in your mind. If those phrases and words still attack you, try to eradicate them immediately with your mental "picture." At first you might feel uncomfortable confusing your intentional images with the "trashy" ones, but if you learn to separate them, you will have no problem in stopping your train of thought.

Exercise "Empty Room"

Imagine that your mind is a room stuffed with scores of things: furniture, books, appliances, and clothes; each of them associated with some event or person in your life. Let's say, the couch is your work, the chair is your girlfriend, the table is your parents, the dishes are your children, and so on. Take all those things out of the room one by one, leaving it absolutely empty.

Then take yourself by the hand and drag yourself out as well, locking the room behind you. The room (your head) is now empty. All you can do is to peek inside through a window, and if some objects appear in the room, you can use a refrigerator magnet to catch and pull them outside.

This drill is pretty similar to the one called Inner Observer, when you have to imagine that you only watch everything that is happening inside your head from outside. The Observer is passive, he never interferes, and he does not participate in producing the internal dialogue—he just watches it closely. As a result, your internal dialogue gets confused because it does not get active support from you, and it eventually ceases.

Please be careful when doing this exercise because creating two separate entities in your brain (Internal Dialogue and Inner Observer) can complicate your selfcommunication, especially if you did not try the first two exercises and just jumped to this one.

Exercise "Dog in a Doghouse"

Imagine that your restless and uncontrollable mind is a dog that should stay in its doghouse at all times, with the exception of when you (the owner) allow it to get out and bark (to think) outside in the yard.

Scan your brain every now and then. Your dog must be in its doghouse and your mind should be silent. If you notice that you are agitated or depressed, or various thoughts are bothering you, you can be sure your dog escaped from the doghouse and is running around the yard on its own. Catch your "Fido" and order him back to his place. Block the entry to the doghouse.

If you do not like the reference to a dog, come up with your own model and use it. The most crucial thing is to learn to control your mind, making it work only when you need it.

Summary

1. Using the Method of Forming Events by Thought Power is best in this order:
   - relaxing your physical body
   - stopping your train of thought on demand
   - detecting and recognizing real life goals
   - enhancing your inner energy and self-assurance
   - achieving your needed results

2. The main three techniques on stopping the uncontrolled of thoughts are the following:
   - technique of focusing your mind on one object/image
   - technique of conscious suppression of thoughts

3. You can use any of these methods or all of them together in order to accomplish the desired effect, which is silence in your head. As a result of these exercises, you will develop skills to enter a state of mind in which you will be able to clearly perceive your egregors' advice.

4.4   Declaring Your Life Goals

Now, when you know how to calm down your mind and are able to recognize the hints of your egregors, you can go ahead and use your new abilities to make your wishes come true. For this, it is better to follow a certain "schedule" in mind, especially in the beginning.

Detecting Authentic Life Goals

First you have to decide what you really want—in other words, which hill you need to climb right now. It is imperative to do it, so you don't get offended with Life later on because it didn't fulfill your dreams. Life itself always grants us what we fancy, but very often we do not even know exactly what we want. To be more precise, it turns out that our mind wishes for one thing, yet our soul wishes for something else. Life will only bequest upon you what your soul desires.

How does it work? For instance, you are sincere in your desire to find a new job and earn more money, but deep inside you fear that you are not qualified or that you are not of the appropriate age. Now you know that it is called an idealization (that is, exaggeration) of your own imperfection. This exact fear is, in fact, your real order that Life takes from you: "I don't want any change because I even do not know what I am doing at my present place of work. I am afraid; leave me alone." Life identifies this hidden notion and makes your languorous job search invalid right there, and you do not move in any way toward your "goal." Guess why—because your authentic wish not to change anything was granted.

Another example, a girl tries to find herself a husband or a loved one, and she is getting really upset that she is failing at meeting the right person. Yet, she has fears inside her soul of being cheated on, as had happened to her in the past (or to her girlfriend), or she is afraid that she would be a bad wife or that the man would restrict her freedom and would ill-treat her. This hidden fright sends Life a message: "I don't want to be married! I am afraid," causing no alternative for her to meet a new man.

Let's say an old lady wants to get rid of her serious illness and makes an immense effort to find new medicine and treatment for it. In reality, her sickness is a form of manipulating her relatives, whom she constantly accuses of being the reason for her health condition. If she finds the cure, then she will lose the instrument for controlling her surroundings, and subconsciously, she cannot allow this to happen. Since her illness gives her advantages in her family life, the nature of her wish for good health is inauthentic—thus, Life keeps her unhealthy.

So, you can clearly see that our really *true* wishes often differ from the ones we openly declare, and that Life awards us only with the true ones. If you distinguish your authentic desires and separate them from the false ones, you will better understand your present situation.

Recognizing your authentic wishes can be done differently.

You can once again analyze your current life and see all the advantages/disadvantages. Try to understand whether, in your wishing for a particular thing, you are serving your soul or rather the impulses of your relatives, friends, or colleagues. If you use good logic, you will definitely come to the right conclusion and detach your true wishes from the erroneous ones.

You can also address your concerns on this matter with a professional—for example, your psychologist. Another option is to use the help of your egregor, listening to his tips and hints, or get an answer through so called "automatic writing," which will allow you to receive information straight from your subconscious.

Exercise "My Authentic Goals"

For this exercise you will need a piece of paper and a pen.

Sit down at a desk, in a quiet place where other people will not disturb you (disconnect your phone and turn off the television and radio). Take the pen and position your hands on the desk so that at any moment you will be able to start writing. Relax your body and empty your mind.

Ask yourself mentally: What are my authentic wishes? What do I truly want to achieve?

What are the main obstacles? etc.

Then you have to wait calmly for some thoughts (words, phrases, or images) to enter your mind. You do not need to ponder your questions or drastically try to answer them; all you have to do is wait.

When the thoughts start to appear in your head, you need to write them down one by one. If you manage to tune yourself appropriately, your subconscious will give you from five to fifteen different answers during a ten- totwenty-minute period.

When writing down "the answers," please exclude any judgment, interpretation, or comparison; neither should you turn on your internal dialogue. Just entrust yourself to the whole routine, and you will get a valuable record on the piece of paper that might include very clear answers, as well as abstract ideas.

Whatever will come up in your head, being at times very chaotic, do not be afraid of it. Quite often, especially in the beginning, people get "junk mail" because their energy channels are so littered with mental gibberish. In the course of time, the channels will clear up, and you will start receiving consistent, precise information on the issues in question.

After having recorded your five to fifteen answers, you can come back to your natural state of mind (turning on your logical thinking and criticism) and try to figure out the writing. Perhaps this information will match everything you already know, opening no new horizons.

In this case, it will be a good sign that you have already been actively using the hints of your egregor, and he does not have anything new to tell you at this time.

Yet, very often, the answers received during the "automatic writing" differ a great deal from what you are used to thinking about your own being. Do not rush to throw them away in disagreement. Try to keep them for a couple of days and think about them. Most likely, if you are honest with yourself, you will find grains of truth in the writing, and you will be one step closer to the final happy result.

When doing this exercise, it is important not to confuse your internal dialogue with the voice of your subconscious.

The process should only be carried out according to the formula: *silence—question— answer—silence.*

What to Do with Your Authentic Goals

Really, what are you going to do with your fears and apprehensions, which you tried to hide for so long, but which have manifested themselves in your "automatic writing"? You have to realize that it was those fears that were actually blocking your way to success.

Make a conscious choice about what is more important to you. Do you value your freedom or marriage with its obvious restrictions; your peace of mind at your present job or a higher-paying position with all the responsibilities that come with it; your health or your desire to nag your relatives at any cost?

Make your choice and relax. You can select a smaller salary and your peace of mind, and it will be a reasonable choice if you are sure that money is not worth a nervous breakdown. And vice versa: You can choose a higherpaying job in a package with a tense environment if you feel that you are missing that cutting edge.

A girl should decide whether it is more important for her to be free and manage her time on her own, or to get married and sacrifice her freedom. If she chooses marriage, then she should consciously look forward to losing part of her freedom for her loved one. Whatever choice you make, do it with joy and an open heart, and Life will reward you for your audacity.

Turning your life into a series of disappointments and contemplations about the quality of your choice will result in producing new idealizations, leading to the most distressing consequences. Take it for granted that all your decisions are correct to begin with—you cannot be wrong because you consulted with the Highest Powers in existence.

Do not pay much attention to what other people say about your decisions. You are destined for success!

Let Life Know about Your Choice.

Here comes the time to tell Life (and your egregors) exactly what you have selected out of the wide range of your desires and wishes.

The Second Principle of the Method states: "Climb only one hill at a time"—that is, prioritize your goals and focus on the most vital one.

If you remember about the Second Principle, then you have to choose only one goal and focus on it, which is somehow hard for all of us to do. A person who is focused on one goal only is called a fanatic. He is usually an outcast of society and can only exist among his peers.

Religious fanatics only talk and think about God—nothing else is of any interest to them. Gambling fanatics are only concerned about gambling and winning. Drug addicts (fanatics of extreme sensations) only care about drugs. Sports fanatics consider sports their only life, etc.

We are far from considering here the problems of such people. We would like to focus on ordinary people with their urges to have a better job, a loving family, a nice house, educated children, good health, etc. So which hill does a regular person have to climb to start with?

Try to choose what worries you the most at present and regard this problem as your "first hill." By no means should you forget about your secondary goals, just build them consistently within the same "mountain range."

For instance, your goal in the professional area is declared to be: "I want an income of
$50, $100, or $200 thousand a year." Pick the income that would

match your real abilities and make efforts to get it. On the other hand, if Life has money enough for everybody, then why not to ask for more? The important thing is that you should *not ask for income that is more than five times bigger than your present one*; otherwise, you yourself would not believe that you are worthy of this money. You might develop an internal fear, which can block your ability to increase your income. But thinking about doubling your salary would seem like a pretty achievable idea. After raising yourself by this one step, you can later set up a goal to increase it again, and so on.

This recommendation does not imply that you are not worthy, and that Life is stingy. Life would eagerly give it all to you, but you yourself would not take it without trusting that it could be yours by right. Only few people have this self-confidence and have courage to order lots of money, and they have a chance to get it if they arrange their "order" in a correct manner. These people are the ones who climbed their career ladders in no time, be it in show business, financing, or science. They also have their "steps," which are bigger than those of ordinary people.

For the rest of us, we recommend warming up and accelerating little by little. Undoubtedly, a very important area of our lives is our family—*love, partners, and children.*

If in this area you have particular wishes, please, shape them very accurately: "I am getting married to a rich person who loves me and whom I love," "My relationship with my husband/wife is improving," "I am meeting the person of my dreams and we are going on a wonderful trip," etc.

The same should be done in regard to your health problems: "I am finding a doctor that helps to cure my long-term illness," or to your hobbies: "I am submitting a great work of art and am getting recognition for it," or to your personal abilities: "I am easily learning a new language within six months," and others.

Write down your goals on a piece of paper in order of their priority, enter them in your electronic organizer, or make it a screensaver on your computer— the idea being you have to see this list every day and read it over and over. This way the reminder will be sent to your egregors about your intentions all the time. You can draw a picture of your goal or make a photo collage and place it on the wall, so every time you look at it you get the pleasure of imagining that this goal is already achieved. Whatever you decide to do, make sure you remind yourself about your wishes and desires every day, and experience only positive emotions when thinking about them. By doing so, you will drag the attention of the higher egregors to your goals, and they will further protect you from experiencing any negative feelings in regard to your wishes (fear, inferiority complex, panic attacks, disappointments, etc).

At this stage you can use all your knowledge in marketing, planning, financing, managing, and other aspects of practical activity. Planning is a process of "ordering" Life to supply you with what you need/desire.

By pondering different aspects of your plan and coming up with ideas on how to execute it, you will focus your thoughts on the very essence of your goals, which will help your egregors produce the results you need.

Once again, we would like to remind you to be positive. Even when considering possible obstacles within your plan, you have to be inventive in finding positive ways out.

Besides, do not forget about the Seventh Principle:

"God has only your hands." It is you who has to act, and then your egregors will form the desired event.

Requirements When Shaping Your Goal

There are certain rules to follow when defining your life goals. If you break them, then the result can be different from what you had expected. These rules are quite simple, and they will keep you from making mistakes.

First, when you declare your goals and wishes, *you should only refer to yourself.* Do not include your relatives, friends, or even loved ones. They all have their wishes that probably do not match yours. For instance, you should not shape your wishes in this way: "My child becomes a good student." "My husband starts making lots of money." "My mother stops interfering with my life." etc.

It is not going to happen because those people are not wishing to change. An order like "I am making lots of money and am helping my parents" also does not have many chances of succeeding because, as a matter of fact, your parents did not ask you to make lots of money for them.

Life only performs *what you intend for yourself.* When figuring the formula of your order, you have to include the words "I" and "for me"—otherwise, your order will not include you.

Secondly, *do not use negative words* like "not," "no," etc.

Ask for what you want without trying to get rid of what you have. Your order "I do not want to be sick" will not work. It is clear that you do not want to be sick. Then what do you want instead? There might be various implied answers, whether you realize it or not—for instance, "I want to die." So if you want to be healthy, just say, "I want to be healthy."

Use these recommendations, and Life will give you want you need. If you face difficulties, then re-evaluate the consequences of your wishful thinking, and try to see if you have some hidden desires that actually block the way for the desires you openly declared to come true.

Typical Mistakes When Shaping Your Goals

One of the mistakes lies in breaking the Second Principle of the Method: "Climb only one hill at a time." We are all tempted in our lives, and we want to get everything *right now.* As a result, we seem to be running in all possible directions at the same time. We want to enjoy what we do professionally, love and be loved, have houses and cars, get elected, be recognized, be awarded, hit the lottery, etc.

Trying to work out all those wishes at the same time take lots of energy, leaving no chance of achieving them to the fullest extent possible.

In our Method, we call it *uncertainty of the purpose of your goals*. You have the right to desire everything at the same time, but keep in mind that you will not have energy to "pay" for the implementation of your wishes.

Another mistake concerns setting up *unrealistic goals*.

For instance, you wish to become President of your country. If you do not have a college degree and have fear of public speaking, this goal is impossible; trying to achieve it in any visible future seems unreasonable; and no system, including our Method, will help you. If you set up this type of goal, Life will not help you to execute it, thereby protecting you from stress and trauma. Choose real goals and you will have a good time in the process of reaching them.

Another mistake is to place an *inaccurate order*. By declaring, "I want love!" you are expecting that Life will send you a rich, handsome blonde. Life rushes to grant you your wish, but since you did not put your order into detail, and there are no rich handsome blondes in stock at the moment, Life will give you the love of a bum off the street or even the affection of the neighbor's dog. Is this what you asked for?

The same happens with slogans "I want money!" without mentioning what exact amount, etc. You will find a dollar in the street, and Life will wash its hands about completing your order.

So be accurate and precise when declaring your goals; otherwise, you leave loose interpretation to your egregors to figure out what exactly you want. You will get it in a different form or shape, without even noticing it, and you will get disappointed that Life is not sending you what you wish for.

Whatever is happening, have this affirmation: "Each moment of my life. I live in paradise and am happy about what I have created today. I will do my best to shape this paradise more to my liking in the future."

Summary

1. Declare your goals to Life, so it can come to the rescue.

2. *Since Life makes only your authentic wishes come true, you need to recognize what exactly you want. For doing, it you can use different techniques, including talking to your subconscious by performing an "automatic writing" drill.*

3. If you detect a difference between your authentic and false wishes, you have to make a decision which one to choose. Life will be satisfied with either of your decisions, as long as it will bring peace and joy into your heart.

4. Having made your decision, you have to tell Life what you want to achieve in different areas of your being. The number of your goals should not be big; otherwise the completion of those goals can be dragged on for many years.

5. When shaping your intentions and goals, you have to observe certain rules, allowing you to avoid misinterpretations about your goals by your egregors.

4.5   Increasing Your Energy Level

Your mental message should be strong enough to be heard by your egregors; otherwise, it has a chance of getting lost among the billions of requests of other people on this planet wishing for something every single minute.

Helping you to create the feeling of euphoria, and bringing you to a higher level of your own being, which aids in attaining life goals pretty quickly. Unfortunately, it wears out within two to three months, and then people have to do it all over again, becoming addicted to this sort of training.

We offer you yet another system that involves selfwork on increasing your energy potential. You will not be addicted to any official system, and your future will depend only on you.

Building Self-Confidence

The deadline for completion of your goals depends *on the potential of the inner energy* that you have.

If you have a lot of self-confidence and are full of life, then some of your wishes can come to reality in no time. Such people rarely read books like this; they do not need to do so.

If you are reading this book now, it means you have a lower energy level, and you possess some doubts about yourself and life in general. You have to use certain exercises to help you build up your energy level.

Inner Doubts Devour Your Vital Energy.

Your usual thoughts "Did I do it right?" "Maybe I said something wrong." and "Have I made a mistake here?" render a big loss of your power. Your inner doubts, being a result of the uncontrolled work of your mind, lay waste to your health and strength. A person who falls victim to his mind's doubts is hardly well adapted to prosperity in life. His non-stop internal dialogue destroys his potential to embrace great achievements.

It does not mean that we insist upon having no doubts and apprehensions. Having doubts is a very intrinsic part of human nature. We are trying to persuade you to solve your problems with the help of your High Potential, rather than listening to what "voices in your head" tell you.

For this, as we mentioned before, you have to learn to stop your internal dialogue and make some empty space in your mind for answers to your vital questions.

Your Inner Power Guarantees Your Success.

A person holding a strong energy level can contact at will any egregors, including the highest ones, and literally make them implement his plans. Such people are few, and they usually do not pay much attention to their incredible abilities—it comes naturally to them.

Yet, if you possess a very high energy level and still "run in different directions," breaking the Second Principle of the Method, you can wait for a very long time before your wishes come true. And vice versa: If you combine this energy with your authentic and important life goal, your dream can become a reality the next day.

There are different ways to increase your inner power.

You can practice Eastern disciplines of Cigun or Tai Chi, use Yoga breathing exercises, or resort to Rebirthing exercises.

You can charge your inner "battery" from nature—sun, water, and trees. You can do anything that lifts you on a higher energy level.

Choose the appropriate method according to what effect you need to achieve. If you are going on a date and you need courage to say, "I love you," to somebody, then you need a gentle kind of energy.

Nature itself can give it to you: the sunset, for instance.

Exercise "Crystal Vase"

Face a sunset or sunrise. Squint your eyes just enough to see a very thin ray of light coming from the Sun into your eyes.

Acknowledge this ray and then close your eyes. Imagine that your body is an empty crystal vase that has to be filled with the beam of light. Start filling yourself with this sun "liquid" through your eyes, imagining little by little how your whole body (legs, arms, head) gets filled by the sun till it starts overflowing over the top of your head (the brim of the crystal vase), creating a shield of light around you.

If it is overcast or you are indoors, you can just imagine a beam of light coming to you from above, "charging" you. After the exercise, "wash" your face with your hands.

You will need yet another exercise if you are called to talk to your boss or business partner and you literally have to impose your point of view on them. For this drill, it is imperative that you are able to be alone because it requires your verbal participation.

Exercise "I Am powerful"

Stand straight, raise your hands to your chest, make fists, and swing them up or down or to the sides, whatever you feel like.

At the same time, say or shout emotionally and loudly: "I am powerful! I am all energy! I am the owner of my own life!" or "I am happy (rich or successful)!" Your phrase can contain a practical message: "I am the manager of my department!"

"My report is the best!" or "I am attractive to everybody!"

Do it approximately five to six times in a row. If you put your strength behind it, you will feel the waves of energy coming to your body.

This drill gives you a firm kind of energy needed by military people, managers, politicians, and other people who want a career uplift or higher salary. You can do this exercise several times a day, especially before important meetings or professional gatherings.

Learn Your Own Self.

The next step in the process of increasing your energy level will require your understanding of what kind of person you are. You will need to remember how many "mountaintops" in your life you have already conquered and acknowledge yourself for those achievements.

We have to note here that many people do not recall their successes often and tend to underestimate their achievements in life, which is a definite no-no.

Exercise "My Achievements"

Take a piece of paper and a pen. Divide your piece of paper into three sections, giving a title to each of them:

1. "My positive character traits"
2. "What did I achieve?"
3. "How can I manifest myself better?"

Take a comfortable seat at a table, relax your body, and calm down your internal dialogue.

Ask yourself in your thoughts about your good character traits, and start writing your answers in the corresponding table. The list can be as long as you wish, including kindness, perseverance, the ability to comfort people, sincerity, etc., as well as your skills, like knowledge of foreign languages, ability to draw wonderful paintings or play a musical instrument, and others.

The experience shows that even the most modest person can dig out of himself about a dozen positive traits of character.

Don't be shy to use as many pieces of paper as you need.

When you finish with the first table, start filling the second one. Do not pay attention to your internal dialogue, as it will try to take an initiative and interrupt your concentration. You have to write down all your achievements in life, no matter how insignificant they might seem to you at the moment. It can be graduating from college, marriage or divorce, an interesting trip or purchase, meeting a fantastic person, writing a song, or catching a big wish.

When you deplete your memory on this account, move to the third table, and fill it in the same way. The range of the answers can be very wide, as well. Maybe you would want to be a general, a renowned politician, a spy, a father of ten, or a playboy. It is good if the writing in the second and third tables somehow crosses and complements each other, meaning you do not just write your fantasies in the third table, but base them on the particular life achievements that hold the promise that your fantasies are possible.

In this manner, any person can find five to ten activities in which he can definitely succeed, provided he is persistent at them.

This exercise requires fifteen to thirty minutes of your time. After you are done, come back to your natural state of mind and read what you have written. We are sure you will be surprised to see all your merits and achievements.

People are very often conditioned to underestimating their own accomplishments and focusing on their own shortcomings.

Over time, this negative self-talk lowers their energy level, self-confidence, and motivation.

This exercise gives you a chance to re-evaluate your self-opinion and bring your self– esteem up to a healthy, positive level.

Do not discard your writings. You can continue doing this exercise by adding new accomplishments to the file.

As you continue to do so over time, you'll find your selfworth naturally becoming more and more reinforced.

Your level of confidence increases to an appropriate and healthy degree, thus forwarding you the pursuit and achievement of your desired goals.

It is important to remember while doing this changework that people around you are also outstanding and worthy in their own ways. Looking down on others can result in generating a new idealization (exaggeration) of your own talents. If this occurs, Life has a way of teaching you a lesson.

The best motto to adopt is this: "I am a super being! All people around me are super beings!"

Summary

1. *The deadline for carrying out your desires and wishes strictly depends on your accumulative energy within. Your dedication to increasing your energy level and self-esteem by all positive means available works as an energy booster. The first step is to get rid of your fears and doubts.*
2. *Visual imagery is a powerful tool you can use to enhance your motivation and belief. It helps to visualize your goals in as much detail as possible.*
3. *For increasing your self-confidence, it is necessary to put in writing your previous achievements and continue adding to the list.*

4.6   Achieving the desired results

The last stage of the Method of Forming Events by Thought Power deals with your acknowledgement of what Life is giving you. You simply generate a pleasant feeling of satisfaction *as if your dreams already came true.* By doing so you create a whole realm of Being Happy before your goals are accomplished.

There is nothing new in this statement. It has been stated in many sources over the ages that, if you want to become a millionaire, it is necessary to *feel as if you are a millionaire* right now. Think, walk, breathe, look, and behave like a rich and successful person. Of course, this does not mean spend like one—more so, the emotional state is what you are seeking to emulate. The money and opportunities will manifest if you play this role truthfully for some time. Before you know it, your company will offer you a promotion, your partners will trust you on challenging projects, or other "miracles" will happen bringing more abundance into your life.

We already told you about the lady who got pregnant against all odds because she just created a state of being pregnant in her mind. If you are looking for a loved one, you have to feel as if you are already being with him/her, and life will arrange for you to meet one another.

Think Well about Yourself.

If you doubt yourself all the time, this thinking reflects in your eyes, energy, and actions. People around us can sense low self-esteem and respond accordingly. They will not offer someone a higher position at work if they feel that they are not content with themselves.

Create and maintain an image of what you want to be in your life. Our exercises will help you do this fast.

To start with, you have to find out what you are still lacking—that is, what inner qualities you will need to develop to compliment your outstanding persona.

In addition, try to uncover what limiting belief patterns hold you back, or aspects of character or behavior that stand in the way to your happy life.

Exercise "My Qualities"

Take a piece of paper and divide it in two. Title the left part "Traits of Character I Want to Lose." Title the right one "Traits of Character I Want to Develop."

Relax your body and let go of your internal dialogue. If it persists, just observe it without judgment and continue with the exercise. Ask the questions stated. Write the answers you receive in the corresponding tables. You will be flooded with statements that you need to lose weight or calm down your temper, that being bold or having an ulcer hampers you from success, that you should be more courageous or attractive or dress differently, etc. All these answers are valid provided they concern only you, rather than the circumstances of your life.

When the answers stop arriving (within ten to fifteen minutes), come back to your natural state, and review the notes. You will see that you now have compiled a list of all your shortcomings and merits, as well as created a deeper understanding of what traits of character, beliefs, and behavioral patterns you would like to develop. Sit quietly with this information for a few moments. The following exercise is going to help you *generate the necessary qualities.*

Exercise "My Role Model"

From the list that you generated in the course of the exercise "My Qualities," choose two to three traits of character that you want to develop in yourself.

Now spend a minute or two bringing to mind a person who possesses these qualities. It could be your friend or relative, as well as your favorite actor or well-known politician. If you cannot come up with a real person like this, just make up or create this ideal person in your imagination. Visualize how he walks, dresses, talks, etc.

Now imagine that it is this person who has to deal with your day-to-day issues and problems. Run through your mind different scenarios of how this ideal man/woman deals with your life issues. See or imagine them making the right decisions and attaining everything they set out to do. Now put this ideal image onto your own being, as if you are putting on a jacket.

Try to feel, walk, talk, and laugh like him. Be this ideal, capable person in your mind. Find the imagery that feels best to you.

This technique is actually very similar to an actor's rehearsal process when they are creating/discovering the inner qualities of a character role they are to play. The only difference is that an actor cannot change the plot. You can!

As the creator of the plot, you can create the circumstances for this ideal person. You are the actor, screenwriter, director, and audience all at the same time.

Do this exercise as often as you want *till you feel comfortably "reincarnated" into the image of your role model.* Do not worry if you feel that you need to create an image of a scandalous and difficult person in order to reach your specific goals.

That is perfectly okay. This process brings fascinating discoveries. Just play this game called "Life Is a Play."

When you learn to play this role, begin playing with it in real life. Start putting on the ideal image every time you need to demonstrate a set of those particular qualities. In your mind it will be the ideal person who will act, and *you*, in your turn, will *only execute* their decisions and will. This ideal person will be responsible for everything, so you can give him freedom to choose what is best for you. Of course, these choices are within the parameters of our established legal system and ethical codes. Your ideal person is a person of integrity.

Changing Circumstances of Your Life

Taking into consideration all the knowledge about the Method of Forming Events by Thought Power, the question of whether we ought to influence others arises.

In other words, should we try to disconnect other people from one egregor and connect them to another?

It can be tempting. For instance, you want to make your husband/wife stop drinking (that, is to disconnect him from the low-level egregor of alcoholism). Or your child starts doing drugs, and you wish you could divert him/her from this dangerous habit. Perhaps your loved one does not want to get committed to the relationship, and you do.

There are many situations like this that we would like to change.

If you are reading this book right now, it means that everything you tried before failed. Ask yourself this question: Have you created a model of this world in your mind that differs a great deal from what is in reality? Are you constantly trying to adjust the real world according to the perfect picture in your head, and thus experiencing a range of negative emotions? Do you ever feel guilty or ashamed because you think you somehow failed?

Perhaps it was like this before you started reading this book. Now you have the tools and the knowledge to eliminate this pattern of thinking and feeling. Now you can accept the truth, know that you have the right to create this ideal model in your mind, and install goals you had perhaps previously judged as impossible.

The key element in this system is the following: It does not matter what you do and imagine; it matters *how* you do it.

Having self-confidence, forgiving yourself for mistakes, and finding the lessons in them, or breaking through closed doors, walking on people, killing your integrity, and ignoring all the signs that Life is sending you? If you choose the second way, Life (via egregors) will teach you a lesson.

Walking the path to your goals, you should acquire a flexible technique of sensible Way of Being and take an appropriate life position (remember, Life is a Game).

If you do it, you will find peace of mind that you will be able to share generously with your family, friends, and loved ones. Let's say you managed to find this peace of mind and feel serene right now.

At the same time, your spouse still drinks, the child still experiments with drugs, and the loved one does not propose to you. It seems that you are losing in this game, and you would like to turn it into a victory.

Now how can you change this situation using the Method of Forming Events by Thought Power?

We already mentioned that our Method works effectively when you apply it to solve problems concerning only you personally (increasing your income, finding a spouse, etc.).

It is less effective when you try to influence other people to make decisions that will help you to reach your goals. You may still try to do it, however, so we have a couple of recommendations for this.

Influencing the Surrounding World

If you are still determined to influence another person, stick to the following rule: *influences the environment of this person, not the person himself.*

If you want your spouse to stop drinking (see the examples in the previous paragraph) without him/her having the same wish, you should attempt to build a certain mental model of the development of the desired event.

By doing so you will find yourself in the middle of a battle with the egregor of alcoholism, fighting to sever his ties with your spouse. If you possess powerful energy, most probably you will succeed. If not, you risk defeat in this fight. The rule we stated above suggests *a way to overcome this.* Now create in your mind a model of a *new situation* where your spouse simply would not be able to drink. It could be moving to a new place, a serious business trip, visiting very religious relatives, getting involved in a new hobby, etc. Choose your model and use all your positive energy to transfer it to real life. Then your egregors from the Subtle World will help you to create this new reality, doing business as usual (instead of fighting you).

This rule can be applied to almost all situations in life. It is very hard to inspire or cause another person to love you when he/she is not interested in you at all. It is easier to create an environment where he/she *will have to maintain stable communication with you on an everyday basis, getting a chance to discover your great personality.* Then you can use all your charms to attract him/her. What happens is this: *You create a situation where the person is compelled to act according to what you want from him/her.* It might take a long time, but it is better late than never.

Do not use the Method for achieving negative goals.

If somebody has wronged you and you just "dream" of getting rid of him, please do not place an order for this person to get sick, get into a car accident, or die. Instead, wish him well. You can imagine that he gets promoted and moves to a different department, or he inherits lots of money in Puerto Rico and moves over there. Wish him anything, as long as it is *a good thing.* You do not have a say in whether this person deserves this good thing. Simply perform an act of mental charity and wait. Time will show what he will get and how the events will unfold— this is the responsibility of a team of miscellaneous egregors, as you already know.

The advantage of this way of behaving is that the higher egregors will hear your virtuous thoughts, they will understand that you wish to be parted with this person, and they will arrange for this. On the contrary, if you create negative models in your mind concerning this person, then you will only get in touch with the low-level egregors, who might be fond of this person. Thus, instead of punishing him, they will turn on you defending their "friend." Your high egregors, in this case, would not be able to protect you because they can perceive only positive thoughts coming from you.

All of the above can be put into one sentence: *When forming events concerning other people, only focus on positive courses for these events.* If you do not break this rule and use correctly all the instruments of the Method of Forming Events by Thought Power, then the probability of the planned wish will be very high.

Summary

1. At the very last stage of using the Method, you have to once more to show Life your positive notion about achieving your desired goals. You should try to create a state of being in which you already have what you want.

2. For building higher self-esteem, it is recommended to create an Ideal Person in your mind that possesses all the essential qualities of the character needed for making your wishes come true and learn how to "play" his role whenever necessary.

3. If you want to help another person, do not push him into doing what you consider reasonable, but rather create an environment where he will change his behavior to your liking.

4. When creating situations for other people, only wish them success and prosperity.

4.7 Safety Precautions While Using the Assistance of the Subtle World

While Using the Assistance of the Subtle World From one perspective, everything that we have offered in this book may sound like just another psychological theory. In short, we recommend focusing on one goal in life: proceeding with a smile. You may read of similar notions in dozens of other books on self-improvement and psychology, which considers itself a materialistic science.

On the other hand, we talk in this book about hardly explainable concept like the karmic educational process, practical interaction with the Subtle World, and egregors. It sounds like mysticism.

So what is it that we are giving you—mysticism, religious notions, or the product of psychological research?

We ourselves refer to this technique of sensible living as untraditional psychology. We title the first section of the Method "Diagnosis of Event's Reasoning."

You should remember that it deals with analyzing the reasons for your present life situation and finding the ultimate way to achieve your goals. You can call this system "positive psychology" because it is geared toward people who want to, and will, think positively.

Nevertheless, our method is not so materialistic. You can come up with various doubts and questions on the moral issues of whether you should use the egregors' help to achieve your personal goals, what is the price you should pay for such help, and others.

Our Method Is a Gumball Machine.

You might say that this Method seems like a gumball machine, where you put a coin in and push a button, and a candy rolls down into your hands, except it does not seem that you are paying. It seems that the Method can give you a candy (house, spouse, money, health, etc.) at no cost.

Yet, your whole life experience causes you to doubt this concept because you know that there are no free lunches, and free cheese can only be found in a mousetrap.

You just know that in order for you to get that candy, you have to put some money (or its equivalent) in a special slot. In short, you have to pay first and then demand the result.

Concerning the Method of Forming Events by Thought Power, it seems that we are offering free cheese: Choose what you want, build a mental model, and get the result. Yet, it only appears this way on the surface.

How We Pay for the Help

So you are carefully looking for that slot in which to pay for your candy. You do not believe that *something can come from nothing*. You are trying to figure out how we pay when using the Method.

The answer is *you are already paying for using the service of your egregors* by your thoughts. Since the egregors feed on our mental energy, they need *you to think about them*, acknowledge them, and inspire other people to use their help.

Our other patron—that we earlier called Guardian—takes care of our soul: He teaches us not to judge people and the outside world. If you observe the rule, then your Guardian is interested in encouraging and helping you to reach your objectives.

Getting help from Life itself is a valid concept. Using the Method of Forming Events by Thought Power and observing the rules is safe and effective.

Knock and the Door Will Be Opened to You.

First of all, you can comfort yourself by the idea that asking Life for help is not forbidden— even in religious sources, we find the confirmation for this: "Ask, and it will be given to you; seek, and you will find; knock, and the door will be opened to you. For it is always he who asks that receives, he who seeks that finds, and he who knocks that has the door opened to him" (New Testament, Matthew 7:7–8).

As you can see, our Method is just an application for this teaching. When you start using it, you will fully realize the concept "knock and the door will be opened to you."

You should knock on the doors of the higher patrons, and if you do it correctly, observing the rules, the door will be indeed opened.

Secondly, even without knowing the Method, *you have been using it all along*; the only difference is that you are not getting expected results. You always think about what you need and how to obtain it; you constantly contact (without knowing it) your egregors, making them run in the heavens in vain efforts to fulfill your dreams.

You can be compared to a blind person with multiple sclerosis coming to a mall trying to buy new clothes for himself. He chooses something without seeing it, then he manages to pay, but finally, he walks away forgetting that he actually needs to pick up what he has chosen; he loses his receipt as well. Some diligent store assistants find those receipts and sometimes try to figure out what exactly he wanted to buy and rush after him with the items that they think he has bought. He moves from store to store in the mall in this manner, and eventually he walks out with a collection of things he does not need, or even with nothing at all.

You are that person with disability. The price for your purchase is your thoughts and emotions, and the purchase itself is your constantly changeable wishes.

So if you pay anyway, would it not be prudent to open your eyes and see what you are buying (or want to buy)?

The Method of Forming Events by Thought Power teaches you this.

Safety Precautions When Dealing with Egregors

If you observe several important rules of dealing with your egregors, you will avoid.

Rule One:

Never use you connection with egregors to achieve dishonorable goals.

We already warned you about it in the previous section, when we recommended wishing only the best to other people. If you wish them ill, the lower egregors are always at your service, and they might help you; perhaps your wish will come true.

Yet, you yourself will receive a full load of problems and troubles as a price for your dishonorable thoughts and actions. The lower egregors are feeding on the energy of fear and horror, and they will definitely come back to you if they do not receive their "portion" of fear and disappointment from the person whom you wish ill. As a result, you might get sick, get into a car accident or mugged or beaten up, lose your job and money, etc. The more troubles in your mind you send toward another person, the harsher they will bounce back to you. It is unpredictable what might happen to you; everything depends on the circumstances of the Subtle World and the opinion of your own Guardian, who may decide to punish you, using the egregors as instrument for this punishment.

Do Not Harm by Accident.

Besides the cases of deliberately wishing ill to other people, we would like to talk to you about the situations *when you can harm somebody by accident*, which happens when, in the process of making your own wishes come true, you hurt somebody unintentionally.

Here is an example: Let's say you are a woman, and you are in love with a man whom you want to marry.

Unfortunately, he is already married, and his marriage is stable. Having in your arsenal the Method of Forming Events by Thought Power, you have a good chance to cause him to divorce his wife and marry you. This, however, involves destroying his present family, which could not be accepted with great enthusiasm by his wife.

She may try everything to keep her family together and will curse the destroyer of her family well-being. All those curses will be sent your way, especially if you feel guilty.

Thus, when choosing the plans to implement your goals, try to see the whole picture and *not to hurt anyone*.

You can always find an appropriate decision: You can create a scenario in your mind where the wife of this man falls madly in love herself with another person and decides to divorce her husband.

Rule Two

This rule deals with situations in which you are provoked for a conflict. We have talked a lot in this book about the nature of conflicts and scandals in your life from the point of view of exchanging energy. Now, we would like to give you a different angle.

When you are attacked in any shape and form, you should choose several different strategies.

The most typical reaction would be to enter the conflict and try to defeat the offender. This is what we see in action films when a character is crushing everything in his way and prevailing at the end of the film.

Sorry to say, in life it does not happen this way. When somebody attacks you, most probably he feels strong (being supported by his lower egregors). If you respond to his provocation, you have to be sure that your energy level matches that of the offender. Otherwise, you are doomed to lose badly.

If you do not feel confident that you can win, then *attempt to avoid being involved in this conflict.* There are many tactics to accomplish this: Try to ignore this person in your mind, bring some levity into the situation by telling a joke, or pretend to be dull. In this case, you will avoid getting "hooked up" with the lower egregors, who are waiting for you to get angry and jump into the conflict. They are already there, giggling in the background and anticipating the feast of aggression and rage over which they will be presiding.

Managing to avoid this conflict will cut the pipe that pumps the evil energy of aggression into your body, and it will cause both lower and higher egregors to respect you. The latter *might want to look at you closer and help you in your life.*

So, do not get involved in arguments and conflicts; otherwise, you will not get Life's protection.

If anyone has already forgotten, we would like to remind you that, by experiencing negative emotions, you attract the attention of the lower egregors, who will do anything possible to keep you angry or disgruntled because they feed on your negative energy.

We hope that telling you about the Method of Forming Events by Thought Power has opened new horizons for you inspiring you to incorporate it into your life.

Summary

1. Experience shows that using the Method of Forming Events by Thought Power is an effective mechanism to establish communication between Life and Man when trying to achieve the desired goals. The main gear in this mechanism is egregors, who either help us to make our wishes come true or create obstacles.

2. Life's assistance in getting what you want should be paid for, like any other service. The price for the help is your thoughts, emotions, and the acknowledgement of your egregors.

3. In order to not fall under the influence of lower (negative) egregors, it is imperative to observe the Main Rule of Life: Do not hold any idealizations.

4.8   Some Typical Errors

In conclusion, we would like to answer some questions that can still remain open at this point.

Do We Have the Right to Wish?

You might think: "If everything is so complicated, do I have the right to have any wishes at all? Maybe I should just lower my standards and accept only what Life (God) gives me without my participation?"

Life or God are indifferent as to whether you live in a three-million-dollar mansion or on the street—whether you eat at McDonalds or at an upscale French restaurant—as long as you are happy. You may live in a shack in the middle of the woods in primitive living conditions and be content with life. Or you can be full of anger, disappointment, and hatred, waking up every day in your expensive chateau, only because your neighbors have a slightly better view from their house. Or you can feel great in your expensive house and miserable in your shack.

In short, having or not having material possessions does not make people happier or more miserable. Money cannot buy happiness. (Does that sound familiar?) Yet, our drive to improve our lifestyle increases every day, and it is a natural state for all of us human beings. Life is glad to help us to get any material possessions as long as we feel grateful and peaceful. Thus, we should desire things and anticipate good results. Just do not forget to thank Life for taking care of you.

Difference between an Idealization and a Goal

You might ask: "If I wish for something really badly, would not my goal turn into an idealization at some point?"

If you look at the definition of an idealization one more time, it states that an idealization is an excessive attachment to something that generates prolonged negative emotions. If you wish for something to come into your life but you do not experience any bad feelings about this dream not coming true for some time, you cannot consider your goal an idealization. On the other hand, if on the way to your goal—be it attaining lots of money, love, or power—you meet harsh obstacles and start feeling depressing sensations, then you can be sure—your goal has turned into an idealization, and you will be pushed by your higher teachers to get rid of it. If you regard the obstacles as the signs of Life and adjust to the information given to you, then you will never have problems, having no idealizations. Sooner or later, you will get what you want.

Should You Always Submit?

You next question might be: "The Main Rule of Life tells us that we should accept it the way it is. Does it mean that when they offend, insult, beat me up, or take my money away from me, I should just tolerate it and submit myself? Do I have the right to defend myself?"

You can choose any strategy, as long as it would not result in accumulating a big pool of negative emotions in your soul. You can accept the humiliation if you think that you deserve it and do not want to take revenge. During the Civil War in Russia, the communists closed the churches and executed many priests. These priests, though young, strong, and healthy men, preferred to accept death rather than "sell" their souls, defending their physical life and letting evil feelings into their being.

Thank God you do not have this hard choice to make nowadays. You have the right to defend your honor, your life, and your material possessions by all possible means.

It is important though to do this without hatred but with

kindness in your heart, even with a sense of pity toward the people who cause you harm.

If you see that your partner is in love with money and tries to deceive you every time or take your share, you might choose to take him to court. If you do this feeling pity toward your partner for the fact that money is the only value for him, you yourself will be saved in this conflict. It is natural that you will be irritated and angry (you are not a priest); just cut those negative emotions short and do not drag them through months and years of your life.

Should They Change?

"I was taking offense at my parents (boss, partner, friend) for their behavior for a long time. Now I realize that they were instruments to teach me a lesson, and I stopped reproaching them. Does it mean that, in their turn, they should change and not behave the way they have been?"

No. Nobody owes anything to anybody in this world. Nobody has an obligation to stop being what he is only because you forgave him. He is what he is, and he is not necessarily behaving the way he is to cause difficulty in your life. Maybe, on the contrary, he is trying (in his mind) to defend you and keep you from making mistakes.

He is the product of a combination of a certain upbringing, education, and life experience.

Perhaps their points of view are out of date, but they cannot think differently!

He does not know how to think/live differently.

So why should you take offense at him for living his life the only way he can? You can choose to be thankful to him instead for showing him the difference between him and you.

For instance you criticized your husband for drinking for a long time, which resulted in him drinking more in protest. Now you resigned to let him drink as much as he wants. Consequently, he does not have to prove anything to you anymore, and there is a chance that he may quit drinking. Yet, it is not guaranteed that he actually will. You cannot demand it from him, only on the grounds that you forgave him and stopped nagging him. He might not quit drinking because other people (family, friends, etc.) still condemn him, and he feels that he needs to fight them.

This is not your problem now because you personally have accepted him the way he is. Your problem would be to decide if you want to continue living with this person until the end of your life.

How to Contact Your Egregors

"Since the egregors execute our wishes and dreams, is there a special way or ritual to contact a particular egregor and ask only him for help? For instance, to contact the egregor of gambling in order to win money?"

There are no secret rules or rituals to contact the egregors besides the ones we have already described in this book: the process of purposeful thinking about the subject of your desire. If you think, plan your activity, clearly visualize your goal, and feel positively, then you attract the egregors by your power of thoughts and emotions, and they help you to execute your objectives.

If you are bustling all the time and your thoughts about your wishes are chaotic and short, no serious egregors will pay attention to you. In order to achieve the needed result, you should make an effort to detect your goals and work them out according to the Seventh Principle of the Method.

Is the Method Acceptable for Religious Believers?

Yes, it is, because the Method of Forming Events by Thought Power does not contradict any religious concept existing in our world.

The Method does not include religious rituals, nor does it use any religious attributes. It is a very effective system for self-improvement.

On the other hand, as you may have noticed, the whole first part of the Method presents an interpretation of the well-knowing precept "Judge not, that you be not judged." Our irritation, frustration, and disappointments are a part of judging the outside world, and we should learn to avoid them. The Method also gives practical tools for how to detect your hidden judgments and get rid of them.

This is the end of our story on how to learn the lessons of Life and become its favorite child. We hope you came to valuable conclusions and are on the way of improving your life dramatically. We wish all your dreams come true!

Conclusion

W E HOPE THIS BOOK WILL HELP YOU THROUGH ITS concepts and practical exercises to achieve your goals in life.

Perhaps something in this book caused you to doubt, and some other ideas inspired you. Nobody holds the Ultimate Truth, and we respect your right to have any opinion on the concepts we offer.

If you go ahead and try (*we recommend* it for at least three to five months) to use the Method in your life, you will see your own results based on your own life experience. We are sure you will be amazed and enchanted. If, after trying this Method, you find that it does not work for you, then look for other ways to improve your life and find peace and happiness.

Never stop looking for what will suit you more, and you will finally find the ultimate tool to make your life the way you want it to be.

Exceptions

The book covered general life of regular people with ordinary cases—that is, *typical situations* in our lives.

We did not intend to explain the cases of death of infants and children, people perishing in mass catastrophes, acts of nature, or terrorist acts. It is clear that the majority of people who die under those circumstances do not have their Stress Accumulators full, and nobody punished them for that. Yet, they died before their time (from a human being's point of view).

Not even religious sources can explain why this all happens (if God loves everybody, then why does He allow that?).

So, we are not the exception to the rule. The only thing we know for sure, that if *you* personally keep your SA full at 50% or less, you will have no fear in your heart and nothing bad will ever happen to you—Life will work such that you will be late for a plane bound to crash, you will not get sick in the middle of an epidemic, you will not be selected for an audit by IRS, you will never get a big traffic ticket, and you will not have enemies.

Your Alexander Sviyash www.sviyash.org

www.ingramcontent.com/pod-product-compliance
Lightning Source LLC
Chambersburg PA
CBHW062133020426
42335CB00013B/1201